HOW TO DEFEND THE FAITH
WITHOUT RAISING YOUR VOICE

230·2

First published in 2018
by Columba Press
23 Merrion Square North,
Dublin 2, Co. Dublin
www.columba.ie

ISBN: 978-1-78218-346-4

Set in PT Serif 9.5/14
Cover and book design by Alba Esteban | Columba Press
Printed by Jellyfish

HOW TO DEFEND THE FAITH WITHOUT RAISING YOUR VOICE

Civil responses to Catholic hot-button issues

MICHAEL KELLY & AUSTEN IVEREIGH

columba
press

ERRATUM

Please find a corrected Table of Contents below.

Contents

Foreword

Archbishop Eamon Martin
Primate of All-Ireland

St Peter urges Christians to "always have your answer ready for people who ask you the reason for the hope that you all have. But give it with courtesy and respect and with a clear conscience" (I Peter 3:15-16). That advice is as relevant today as when the Apostle gave it to the first followers of Christ. In fact, it is arguably more important today in a world of rapid communication where a story can circle the globe in a microsecond.

Before he returned to the Father, Jesus entrusted to his Church the missionary mandate to "go make disciples of all the nations" (Matthew 28:19). While the context changes in every era, the challenge always remains the same: how does the Church communicate the unchanging truths of the Faith in a world that often seems in constant flux?

In his message for World Communications Day 2018, Pope Francis reminds us that "Communication is part of God's plan for us and an essential way to experience fellowship".

The Holy Father goes on to warn that "in today's fast-changing world of communications and digital systems, we are witnessing the spread of what has come to be known as 'fake news'.

"The effectiveness of fake news," Pope Francis notes, "is primarily due to its ability to *mimic* real news, to seem plausible. Secondly, this false but believable news is 'captious', inasmuch as it grasps people's attention by appealing to stereotypes and common social prejudices, and exploiting instantaneous emotions like anxiety, contempt, anger and frustration. The ability to spread such fake news often relies on a manipulative use of the social networks and the way they function. Untrue stories can spread so quickly that even authoritative denials fail to contain the damage".

The Church has often suffered from a distortion of its core teachings in the mass media. Sometimes this is wilful, more often than not it is due to ignorance or the absence of the Church in the public sphere to articulate what it believes and why it does so.

I have often met Catholics who complain to me about false carica-
tures of their faith in the media. Often they feel powerless to present the
Church's teaching or feel that they have an inadequate grasp of the Faith.
How to Defend the Faith Without Raising Your Voice sets out to address that
perceived deficit.

The book aims to give Irish Catholics a new way of talking about
their Faith around the dinner table or with their work colleagues, getting
across the Church's positions on contentious issues without losing their
cool. It's about learning the principles that allow you to step outside the
negative frames sometimes imposed by the news media and being well
briefed on what the Church actually thinks about politics, gay people,
marriage, women, sexual abuse and other key topics.

The approach advocated is about winning friends, not arguments. It is
about shedding light, not heat. Essentially, it's about reframing the argument so hearts can be opened and minds can be inspired.

How to Defend the Faith Without Raising Your Voice is a new approach
to what the Church has often called apologetics. But it is much more than
memorising rote answers to frequent questions – all evangelisation rests
on an individual encounter with Christ, and Christians can only bring
others to Christ by emphasising that encounter.

This book also emphasises that Christianity is a radical 'yes' to a message that is positive rather than a prohibitive set of rules and regulations
aimed at restricting freedom. As the great Pope St John Paul II repeatedly pointed out, embracing the Gospel takes nothing away from us, but
brings ultimate freedom in Christ.

When Pope Benedict XVI visited Spain shortly after his election in
2005, it was in the context of a tense relationship between the Church
and State in Spain. The government had liberalised abortion laws and restricted the teaching of religion in schools, and many media analysts had
predicted that the visit would be a showdown. Benedict instead emphasised the life-giving nature of Catholicism throughout the visit. Bewildered, journalists on the papal plane on the way back to Rome asked the
Pontiff why he hadn't been more confrontational. "Christianity, Catholicism," the Pope replied, "isn't a collection of prohibitions. It's a positive
option. It's very important that we look at it again, because this idea has
almost completely disappeared today.

"We've heard so much about what is not allowed that now it's time to say: we have a positive idea to offer...everything is clearer if you say it first in a positive way," Benedict said.

This positive outlook must be at the heart of our catechesis, evangelisation and outreach. Whether read in groups or alone, studied in schools or parishes, *How to Defend the Faith without Raising Your Voice* offers thorough briefings on hot topics and top tips for effective communication. Michael Kelly and Austen Ivereigh deserve credit for this worthy and much-needed initiative.

Introduction

When the first edition of *How to Defend the Faith without Raising Your Voice* came out in 2012, its first words resonated with many Catholics who found themselves caught in the headlights. "We know how it feels," it began, "finding yourself suddenly appointed the spokesman for the Catholic Church while you're standing at a photocopier, having a drink at the pub, or when a group of people suddenly freezes, and all eyes fix on you. 'You're a Catholic, aren't you?' someone says."

"'Ah, yes,' you confess, looking up nervously at what now seems to resemble a lynch mob. The Pope has been reported as saying something totally outrageous. Or the issue of AIDS and condoms has come up. Or the discussion has turned to same-sex marriage. And here you are, called on to defend the Church by virtue of your baptism, feeling as equipped for that task as Daniel in the den of lions. 'Go on,' they seem to say, but don't actually put it that way. 'Justify what the Church teaches!'"

Not long after the book came out, the world's bishops gathered in Rome for a synod on the 'new evangelisation' - the very particular challenge of offering the Christian message in cultures such as that of Ireland and other parts of the traditionally Christian, Western world. These are cultures that think they know what the Church has to say and believe it is no longer relevant or true. Catholic Voices, the project that gave rise to the book, was praised in the course of the synod as an example of a new approach that sets out to tackle this challenge head-on, by allowing ordinary Catholics to deal with it not as a threat but as a precious opportunity, whether in media interviews or while sitting having a coffee with friends.

The book, like the project, had a simple message: when the spotlight of controversy comes our way, don't shun it. See it as an opportunity. When the Church is in the news, people are interested, curious, amazed, indignant — even scandalised. You have their attention. Learn how to use the moment. Don't look for a hole to dive into, but get prepared.

That's what this book was for. In distilling the methods and insights of Catholic Voices and applying them to the 'neuralgic issues' - where Church and contemporary society clash - *How to Defend the Faith with-*

out Raising Your Voice proved hugely helpful to thousands of Catholics, whether lifelong committed Massgoers or young people exploring a nascent faith who found themselves pinned up against a wall at university. It has also helped build bridges between Christian communities looking for loving and convincing ways to make their case on a whole host of issues — and even their right to exist as Christians and Christian communities outside of the four walls of a church — to a culture that sees them as stuck in the past.

This new Irish edition has been published because, while many things remain the same as they were in 2012, some things are very different. A few topics have waned, while others have come to the fore. The extensive revisions and updates of this new edition better reflect the issues of the day. But it also takes into account a major new factor in the interaction of the Church and contemporary society. His name is Francis.

Pope Francis was elected in March 2013, just a few months after that synod on the new evangelisation, a theme he took up in his apostolic exhortation of November 2013, *The Joy of the Gospel*. There he said the times called for "new approaches and arguments" and "a creative apologetics which would encourage greater openness to the Gospel on the part of all".

In his extraordinary capacity to touch the hearts and minds of people distant from the Church, Pope Francis himself has been a great model of the "new approaches" the synod called for.

He has modelled not just a new means of papal communication, but new ways of speaking about the Church and its teachings that are in reality very old ways. These are the ways of the pastor and the missionary throughout the ages, who begin by speaking first to people's anxiety and longing, their pain and their desire, and the news that a merciful God — one who has a heart for those who suffer — seeks their healing and liberation. "The proclamation of the saving love of God comes before moral and religious imperatives," as Pope Francis put it in an interview in September 2013, before adding that too often in the Church we get this the wrong way around.

The Pope has nailed something important. It's the reason Catholic Voices started in the first place.

The Catholic Voices Story

Ask practising Catholics to tell you about their Church and their faith, and on the whole, you get glowing reports. There will be complaints, and stories of inadequacies, and reservations about this or that teaching, and no one knows the faults of the Church — collectively, and in this or that place — better than those who actively belong. But Catholics will also tell you that the Church is a place of love and welcome, of growth and healing, of support and nurture, of wisdom and of grace, of unconditional acceptance which plays a key role in bringing forth a more humane, caring world. Here's the great, unreported story of our time: Catholics love the Church.

Hence their frustration with the very different picture of the Church often portrayed in the media, where it appears dogmatic, intolerant and judgmental, an institution that seeks its own interests, that imposes and excludes. In short: a 'no' instead of a 'yes'.

This disparity between the perception of the Church in society and the reality familiar to those belonging to it is what sparked the creation of Catholic Voices in preparation for the visit of Pope Benedict XVI to Britain in September 2010.

A team of amateur speakers was formed, consisting of 'ordinary' Catholics — students or professionals, with jobs and children and mortgages — who were determined to explain the realities of Church teaching on radio and television.

They were advertised to editors as "media-friendly, studio-ready, and ego-free": happy to be questioned, sympathetic to the media and journalism, familiar with the demands of three-minute live interviews, and keen to put across not their own views but those of mainstream Catholics faithful to their Church. They were 'unofficial but authoritative': operationally independent of the bishops and not their spokespeople, but who had their blessing; well-briefed lay people offering authoritative, faithful commentary. If you wanted to know what the Church believed and taught, you could call them. No matter how thorny or controversial the topic, they would be there — happy to comment on, debate or discuss virtually any news story.

The project was a runaway success, winning the praise of bishops and broadcasters alike. Having been in dozens of debates and news programmes on radio and television, appearing on all the major British channels, Catholic Voices helped to change both the coverage of the papal trip as well as the perception of the Church in the British media. Since 2010, it has trained dozens more speakers, appeared on hundreds of news programmes, and given guidance and workshops to many Catholic organisations. The project has spread abroad, to more than 16 countries, including Ireland, and has led to a series of new projects: public speaking programmes, trainings, and workshops.

Using the same model, Catholic Voices Ireland (originally launched as Catholic Comment in 2011) has been offering training to Catholics in many walks of life, as well as Church communicators. One of its key achievements was to prepare a panel of Catholic speakers ahead of the 2012 International Eucharistic Congress in Dublin. Since then, its speakers have participated in media debates across all the national broadcasting stations as well as local stations on issues as diverse as the papal conclave, the death penalty, pop concerts clashing with First Holy Communion, eulogies at funerals, female cardinals and Church-state relations.

At its heart, the project turns on an embarrassingly simple idea: that to communicate the Church in contemporary Western culture, one can't just speak and expect to be heard. There are too many filters that prevent it. In communications jargon, these filters are called 'frames'. To be understood, you first have to learn to step outside the frames imposed by our culture that stop you from being heard. That's called 'reframing,' and Catholic Voices teaches a method that enables anybody to do it.

Pope Francis is the Great Reframer

One of the most iconic moments of his first months as Pope was his famous talk with journalists on the flight back to Rome from World Youth Day in Rio de Janeiro in July 2013, when he was asked a very specific question about a gay man. The quote, "Who am I to judge?" took wings, causing shock and delight in equal measure, and quickly took on a life of its own. As commentators were quick to point out, the quote — "If a person is gay and seeks God and has good will, who am I to judge him?" — was uttered as part of an explanation of the Church's teaching on homosexuality, starting with the call in the *Catechism of the Catholic Church* to overcome the marginalisation of gay people.

But while the message may have been used and distorted by some, it was heard loud and clear by most: God loves and accepts everyone, and the Church seeks to help others overcome discrimination and marginalisation.

It was a message people hadn't been hearing from the Church. They had heard judgment, not mercy. They had heard messages about the role and purpose of sex — reserved for a man and woman, in marriage, as opposed to the 'intrinsically disordered' tendencies of homosexuality — but had missed the words of welcome and acceptance. With those few words, Francis added nothing to Church teaching, but removed a filter that prevented it from being heard, and opened the hearer to revising their preconceptions about the Church. That is reframing.

Francis calls this "proclamation in a missionary key". In *The Joy of the Gospel* he points out the way in which contemporary media filters reduce and distort the Church's message, making it appear as a series of prohibitions, sins and faults, or a form of stoicism or self-denial. Yet "before all else, the Gospel invites us to respond to the God of love who saves us, to see God in others and to go forth from ourselves to the see the good of others. Under no circumstances can this invitation be obscured!" he says, adding that the "greatest risk" facing the Church is that without that invitation "the edifice of the Church's moral teaching risks becoming a house of cards".

Francis' "Who am I to judge?" remark provoked such an explosive reaction because it touched on a powerfully entrenched frame underpinning contemporary society. The prevailing ethics of autonomy give people the right to determine their own future, and regard groups that have experienced discrimination as deserving of special sympathy and status. This worldview dominates among educated, urban populations in Western society, and all messages that originate outside of it are regarded with suspicion, as reinforcing discrimination and exclusion. Because of this filter's pervasiveness, what the Church says on the question of homosexuality gets distorted. Begin your discussion of homosexuality with God's purpose for sex, or the notion of morally ordered and disordered inclinations, and what is 'heard' is an attempt to seek divine sanction for prejudice. All else is filtered out. What follows is a dialogue of the deaf — or a shouting match.

Start by speaking to the moral intention behind that frame, as Francis did, and the effect is disarming. Hearts and minds open. The listening can begin.

What Our Critics Really Believe

In the months preparing for the Pope's visit in 2010, we ran through the list of charges against the Church — helpfully supplied by an ad hoc alliance of humanists, secularists, and gay rights advocates known as 'Protest the Pope' — and asked ourselves not why they were attacking Catholics, but what their attacks revealed about what the protesters themselves stood for. We wanted to know what made them tick.

In each case, we discovered a positive value, a moral value, to which the critic was consciously or unconsciously appealing. We realised that the tragedy of much interaction between Catholics and non-Catholics is that each assumes the other is an enemy of a value, rather than the promoter of a value. Contemporary liberalism, for example, faults the Church for bigotry and intolerance, and it is easy for Catholics to find themselves defending the Church's record, indignant at the unjust charge. But what if we see beyond the attack on the Church and realise that behind it is the affirmation of the values of tolerance, fairness, and inclusion?

One of the myths of our rationalist age is that we start from a blank sheet and arrive, by the testing of evidence, at the truths we hold dear. Yet in reality, the opposite takes place. We develop in childhood a series of moral intuitions that our rational mind then tries to justify. Challenged by those who do not share our values, we tend to dig in; our reasoning mind, like a lawyer, works frantically to rebut the other. We can change our minds and amend our views, but only when we feel safe, when we are with others who we feel share our moral intuitions. In that case, we look to find truth in the others' arguments, even when they challenge our own. A true dialogue can then take place.

The reframing method we developed in Catholic Voices allows us to create that safety, by ensuring that we speak to the moral value held by our critics. Rather than be put on the defensive by the charge against the Church, we look for the positive moral value behind it. And we try to begin our response by connecting with that value, rather than seeking to defend ourselves from the unjust attack. Not only does this make it possible to communicate, to be heard and to have a proper dialogue. It also avoids falling into the trap of attacking our own Christian values.

This came home to us in 2010 when we were preparing for the discussion of one particularly thorny topic. In analysing the issue of condoms in preventing the spread of AIDS, we realised that the Church's critics were unconsciously appealing to Jesus, while defensive Catholics were unwittingly being cast into the role of the Pharisee.

The assumption of the discussion was that condoms were key to reducing the spread of the virus, and that the Church could not permit their use because of its clear teaching against sex outside marriage and against artificial contraception under any circumstances. It was an assumption shared by the media, by the Church's critics, and by many Catholics themselves.

This was the frame: AIDS was at the time the greatest scourge facing the human race. Millions were dying. Given the Church's major role in the education and health care of southern African nations, it could easily play a key part in reducing the spread of the virus by endorsing condom use, yet it seemed to stand by aloof and hard-hearted.

Because of the frame, when Catholics pointed out the key role nuns and Church hospitals played in caring for those dying of AIDS, they were greeted with howls of derision; it seemed an even greater hypocrisy and absurdity to be caring for the dying while not lifting a finger to prevent the cause of the sickness they were treating.

The Church stood accused of putting its moral codes before its duty to humanity, sacrificing innocent lives for the sake of the institution. The value it was accused of violating was that of life itself, which should take priority over rules and institutions — precisely Jesus' argument with the Pharisees.

The irony of this hit us very hard. Watching disastrous interviews with Catholics trying to defend the Church over AIDS, we saw them perfectly fitting the role of Pharisee, and the critic using — however unconsciously — Jesus' point of view. The Catholic hadn't realised the dynamic involved, and was assuming that this was an argument about contraception with someone who advocated lax sexual morality. All the Catholic had to do was utter a few lines about doctrine, and the frame was reinforced.

In reality, moral intuitions were at play. AIDS was a proxy for a deeper question: What comes first? Rules and doctrines, or human lives? Is man made for the Sabbath, or the other way around?

Having taken time to consider the critic's positive intention, however, we were able to start from a different place. Rather than try to defend the Church's views on contraception, we began by affirming that the Church's primary concern is saving life. The question of contraception — a teaching about sexual love in marriage — was barely relevant here; this was an issue not about openness to life in marriage, but the avoidance of death in situations of poverty and despair.

Starting there — with the Church as a "battlefield hospital," in Pope Francis' famous metaphor — we went on to discuss the evidence about the best *means* of doing so in the wider population which were, as the statistics showed, what the Church was promoting: behaviour change through abstinence and fidelity programmes. We had escaped the frame. The Church was not standing on the side-lines, judging; the Church was on the front line in the battle against AIDS, preventing as well as curing, close to its people and determined to save them. We were able to reframe.

By looking at the positive intention behind the criticism, we were able to get out of the mindset of 'How can I justify this?' and ask, 'What is the real source of the disagreement here? What are the values and moral intuitions involved?'

To use another example: The mounting desire for an assisted suicide law reflects, of course, ethics of autonomy and a fear of death. But those who advocate it appeal to the positive intention that people should be spared unnecessary suffering; fail to speak to that intention, and a dialogue of the deaf follows. A Catholic who responds by affirming that life belongs to God alone will reinforce the frame that the Church wants the dying to suffer unnecessarily to appease an irate deity, and furthermore seeks to impose that view on society by pressuring it to resist a law that allows the relief of unnecessary suffering. We're stuck in the frame.

But try the positive intention approach, and all changes. First, while suffering is inevitable in ageing and dying, it is true that no one should experience unbearable pain and loneliness, and it is a scandal when this happens. Catholics don't just believe that; they do something. The Church (not just the Catholic Church) has revolutionised the care of the elderly and dying through the development of palliative care pioneered by the hospice movement. Its best practices are influencing the whole nature of end-of-life care, including in hospitals, even as we know that there's a long way to go. Having agreed on the value behind the positive intention, we are able to discuss the effects of an assisted suicide law on the vulnerable, the elderly, and those living with a disability. They must be the priority for healthcare policy. Indeed, those most strongly resisting the passage of assisted suicide are precisely those who are closest to the dying.

No voices need to be raised, because this is a rational discussion. The heat has gone out of it because we are not attacking or ignoring an essential moral value in the outlook of the Church's critics, but speaking to it and affirming it. And we realise that the reason they criticise the Church is because they believe the Church is in some way antithetical to that value. We have the opportunity, in our conversation, to show them that the picture is very different.

Cherchez la Frame

Some misunderstand reframing as a kind of naïve 'happy talk' approach to the critics of the Catholic Church. In fact, it's the opposite. It starts from a clear-eyed understanding that contemporary society is deeply prejudiced against the Church and imposes on it 'frames,' which are born out of ideology. Having described the first step to reframing — understanding and speaking to the critic's positive intention — we now need make sure we grasp which frames are in play.

The real naïveté, in this case, is to be unaware of those frames. It is to assume that the critic is uninformed, rather than fuelled by a moral passion. It is trying to tell people about nuns caring for those dying of AIDS when the listener is thinking: "But they wouldn't be dying if you had let them use condoms."

Discerning the underlying frames is key to reframing, because you soon realise that the Church's critics are not (mostly) pagan or Buddhist or nihilist, but secularised Christians. The secularisation of the Western world means that people abandon the Church, yet they continue, unconsciously, to adhere to its values — and often appeal (again unconsciously) to those values when they criticise the Church.

How this came to be is meticulously documented in Brad Gregory's *The Unintended Reformation*, which shows how sixteenth-century disagreements within the Christian Church led, by stages, to twentieth-century secularism. By the end of the twentieth-century, growing numbers of people believed the atheistic claim that no religious claims are true yet continued to embrace values historically rooted in Christianity. Having detached those values from the Church, they have made the sovereign individual the ultimate arbiter of doctrine and moral truth in contemporary Western society. Morality is subjective and discovered by scientific inquiry. Yet, at the same time, Western secular morality asserts a universal doctrine of human rights based on an unconscious assumption that human beings are all created in God's image and likeness.

In *The Righteous Mind: Why Good People are Divided by Politics and Religion*, Jonathan Haidt observes how wealthy, educated, urban people in the West — the kind that predominate in universities and the media — often share an outlook quite unlike the rest of the world. In most of humanity, the ethics of divinity (we are created beings, who form part of a God-created world) and the ethics of community (we are members of families, nations, and institutions) shape moral choices. For wealthy Westerners, on the other hand, there is an intense focus on autonomy, the idea that society should be organised to enable the greatest freedom possible for individuals to design their own lives and pursue their goals. Autonomy — freedom from coercion — is, of course, a strongly Christian idea, and it is no accident that it is in Christian cultures that this has appeared.

But while the liberal critique and the Catholic position have a shared moral concern, they clash because, unlike the other two ethical principles, which complement each other and overlap, the moral domain of the ethics of autonomy is "unusually narrow," in Haidt's words — limited to moral concerns about harming others or oppressing groups. So while the liberal-individualist draws on a historic Christian concern for victims and for freedom, he or she sees religion and community as antithetical to its moral goals, as burdens to be shaken off and thereafter resisted.

Understanding this mindset and its narrow moral lens allows us to understand why the Church has come off so badly in the news media, and why the Church's compassion for victims, its concern for justice, and its embrace of the outsider get so little attention.

The frames of contemporary, liberal society — reflected in the media, where on the whole journalists are (conforming to Haidt's description) young, urban and educated — put the Church on the negative side of a whole range of dualities. The Church's role in news stories is usually that of an institution that coerces, oppresses, and imposes, while on the other side are ranked the vulnerable individual and victims' groups of many kinds. The woman seeking an abortion, the cancer patient wanting an assisted death, the childless mother wanting in vitro fertilisation (the list is long) are usually juxtaposed, in news reports, by a representative of the Church appearing to utter a big 'no'.

Only by reframing can we escape those roles. That means understanding not only where the value is shared, but also the limitations and prejudices — the frames — of the liberal mindset, and the role they have cast for the Church.

In most of the issues laid out in the chapters of this book, it is the Catholic's task to broaden the discussion — to introduce moral perspectives that are absent from the liberal-individualist viewpoint, rather than attacking the (usually Christian) moral principles it unconsciously draws on.

That way, we don't need to raise our voices and can help create what Pope Francis calls the 'culture of encounter': a place of dialogue and conversion.

Time to Get Briefed

Learning how to reframe — to identify the positive intention, and to speak to it, while being aware of the frames imposed on the Church by contemporary society — is one part of being an effective communicator. The other is being well-briefed on what the Church thinks and says, and knowing how to express it directly and succinctly.

Each chapter in this book tackles, under a broad heading, a series of topics that often come up in a three-minute conversation at the pub, or a half-hour lunch break discussion provoked by an item on the news. We call these issues 'neuralgic' because they touch on nerve endings, those places in the body that, when pressed, cause people to squeal. In our public conversation, they are the points where mainstream social thinking inhabits (at least apparently) a different universe from that of Catholics. Touch on them, and people get very annoyed. "How on earth can you believe that?" they ask you.

Each chapter begins with a series of challenging, even indignant, questions that lay out the neuralgic points for that issue. After giving a brief overview of the issue, we then give the 'positive intention,' the moral frame of the critic, in order to help you grasp his starting point. It should be easy to identify the moral energy behind the criticism: in arguing for same-sex marriage, for example, it will be values such as love and equality. Our answers must respect those moral values — who wants to argue against love or equality? — while showing that the Church's case does not deny these but includes other important values that need to be taken into account.

The rest of the chapter then digs into the facts and the points you need to grasp to be able to make the Church's case on that issue. We can't tell you what to say — every conversation is different, after all — and it's better that way. Each of us must think through the issue for ourselves. But we can help with the 'reframe' and the 'key messages' — summarising the Church's perspective and ending with some essential points that can be made.

Ten Principles of Civil Communication

In the endless debates, interviews, and discussions we've done in studios, these are ten principles we have found helpful to remember — especially when the heat is turned up. Taken together, they add up to a 'mindset' needed for this work.

1. ***Don't get angry. Reframe.*** To recap: Rather than consider the arguments you are going to face, consider the value(s) they appeal to. Look for the (sometimes buried) Christian ethic behind the value. Which other (Christian) values is the critic ignoring, or has the critic not properly taken into account? What are the frames involved? What role has been cast for the Church in this scenario, and how can we step outside it?

    Reframing tells a different story than what's out there. It only works if you are replacing a false picture with a more authentic one. "False ideas may be refuted indeed by argument," said Blessed Cardinal John Henry Newman, "but by true ideas alone are they expelled." Reframing means, above all, preparing well.

2. ***Shed light, not heat.*** The purpose of our communication is illumination. We are not seeking to convert anyone, or persuade by the force of our arguments (if that happens, thanks be to God!), but to help them understand what the Church stands for and why. We are looking to open up new ways of seeing. Our aim is to create understanding.

    Just as you 'catch' faith by witnessing the lives of people of faith who impress you, so you can catch 'light' in an argument. Stay calm and illuminate.

3. ***Think in threes.*** A time-honoured way of preparing for any discussion is to boil your messages down to three key ones. You won't necessarily get the chance to make them all — or you'll have time to make other ones. But the mind finds three easy to remember — which is why Pope Francis usually makes three points in his homilies. If ever you get lost or taken down a blind alley, they are three friends you can always return to. And if ever things get really bad, you can always say: "Can I just make these three points?" If you've reframed well, the first point will usually speak to the critic's positive intention, and the other two will broaden out the horizon.

4. ***People don't remember what you said as much as how you made them feel.*** The best communication takes place when people feel valued and safe. They bend into each other, seeking to understand and share. It's not just about the lucidity of your arguments; it's also about the effect your words have on others. It is not we who persuade; it is the Truth. Our task is to serve the Truth as best as we can. And we serve that Truth best when we aim for civility, empathy and clarity.

    It is easy to win an argument while losing the chance to communicate. Evaluate, therefore, after each exchange, according to one criterion alone: did I help create a 'culture of encounter' that allowed others to better grasp the Church's teachings or positions? How did I make them feel — uplifted or battered? Inspired or harried? Anxious to hear more or relieved when I stopped?

5. **Show, don't tell.** This foundational principle of good writing applies to communication generally. People prefer stories to lectures, and they are more convinced by experience than abstract argument. Make your points clearly and lucidly, but when you can, supplement them with illustrations — anecdotes from personal experience or hypothetical situations that help people 'imagine' what you are trying to say. Rather than tell someone that the Church assists AIDS sufferers in Africa, tell them about the hospitals and dispensaries in the remotest villages in the African countryside where nuns care for patients in ramshackle huts. Rather than say we need more hospices — which are vague, unknown institutions to most people — paint the picture of places where the dying are helped and reassured, and invite people to imagine what it would be like if we had more of them. Think of yourself not as the spokesman of a remote corporation, but as a delighted disciple with stories and experiences to share. Before each interview, discussion, or talk, ask yourself, 'What's my story?' Then think about the best way of telling it, trying to be concise, punchy, graphic and compelling.

6. **Remember to say 'Yes'.** This is a baseline communication principle, and doubly important when we are making the Church's case — as so often in contemporary society — against something. The Church is against many things, but only because it is for so much more — what needs protecting and enhancing. Experience — of prayer, reflection on Scripture, and centuries of immersion in humanity's deepest struggles — have made the Church an 'expert in humanity'. It offers a series of signposts which highlight the wrong turns and dead ends on the road to human flourishing, both in the lives of individuals and in the architecture of society. The Church says 'no' in order to say 'yes'. Remember always to state what we say 'yes' to.

The Church is not a chastising moral policeman; it is more like Mother Teresa, tending to the world's forgotten and ailing people, or Pope Francis, freewheeling around St Peter's Square with a big grin on his face. Keep those and other images dear to you in mind when you speak of the Church's teaching. That way you won't be a grim reaper, but an angel pointing to a brighter horizon.

7. ***Compassion counts.*** Underneath almost all of the neuralgic issues treated in this book are deeply personal ethical questions: ones of sexuality, dying, illness, belief. It is very likely that the person you are in discussion with has had direct experience of the neuralgic issue, either personally, or witnessed first-hand; or has had an experience of authority and institutions that has left them hurt. You may or may not know that he or she has had that experience; if not, you should assume it. God and the Church are common scapegoats for anger, lightning rods for unfocused frustrations. Being compassionate is about understanding this anger and hurt, and relating to it, as one human being to another. The Church, as Pope Francis says, is above all a mother, not a policeman or a moral scold.

Because the contemporary frame often pits the Church as an unfeeling institution against the experience of the individual, it is common to find yourself expected to fill that role. Step away from that frame by appealing to experience rather than abstraction. Demonstrate your empathy and be a good listener, ready to absorb the anger and hurt. Sometimes, compassion is the most valuable witness we can offer.

8. ***Numbers aren't everything.*** Statistics can appear abstract and inhumane, or as spin; politicians using them are usually thought to be lying. Never rely on facts and figures, but use them to illustrate your main point. When you do, speak in human, clear language: not 33.5% of people but 'one in three'.

9. ***It's about witnessing, not winning.*** People who come to a new way of seeing the world find that a prejudice or preconception is challenged, or even reversed. The universe looks different. We call this 'conversion'. It often begins with a prejudice or conviction coming up against a reality that contradicts it; generally, that reality is a person rather than an idea. Think about the frames contemporary society projects onto the Church, and be the contradiction. Every challenge to us is an opportunity to witness.

The enemy of such a witness is a desire to 'win' and 'defeat'. Rivalry and victory, winners and losers, them and us — this is the mindset of the world; Jesus shows another way. Watch him in the Gospel of John: endlessly harried and challenged, he never responds with aggression or the attitude of the persecuted victim, but stands firm, planted in love. Be what you represent.

10. **It's not about you.** Your fear, self-consciousness, and defensiveness are products of a protesting ego. Think of John the Baptist — a fearless communicator; his strength came from knowing that he was the door through which others could come to Christ.

    Nerves help; adrenalin keeps you focused. But excessive jitters may be a sign of self-consciousness. The ego tricks us into believing that we are the focus. Prayer beforehand is vital (Catholic Voices say the prayer at the end of this chapter), to remember who and what this is for. Ask the Holy Spirit to be with you and to speak through you, and for the grace to be a witness.

    If it goes badly, rejoice! Success has almost nothing to teach us, and failure destroys the illusion that it all depends on us. You are doing God's work; it doesn't hang on a good or bad performance. Evaluate, learn, and get back up.

Finding Our Voice

In a January 2012 address to the US bishops, Pope Benedict XVI called for "an engaged, articulate, and well-formed Catholic laity" that had the "courage to counter a reductive secularism which would delegitimise the Church's participation in public debate about the issues that are determining the future of American society".

Speak or be silenced. The contemporary liberal frame — for reasons discussed in Chapter 2 — makes it ever harder for the Church to speak without being accused of interfering or seeking to impose its views. The context calls for *parrhesia* — apostolic courage, boldness in speaking out.

Pope Francis asked for *parrhesia* in his brief remarks to the cardinals, before the conclave in which they elected him, when he painted a choice between a Church anxiously hunkered in on itself and a Church that boldly evangelised. Evangelisation, he said, "implies in the Church the *parrhesia* to come out from itself...and to go to the peripheries, not just the geographical but also the existential peripheries: those of the mystery of sin, of suffering, of injustice, or ignorance and lack of religion, those of thought and every kind of misery."

When he canonised St John XXIII and St John Paul II in April 2014, he praised "two men of courage, filled with the *parrhesia* of the Holy Spirit, who bore witness before the Church and the world to God's goodness and mercy".

It is the quality Francis believes the Church needs at this time. He has become the most talkative of modern popes for a reason: the pressures to say less — media manipulation, the dignity of the office, the fear of being misinterpreted, the risk of confusing Catholics — come from anxiety. He sees them as temptations of the bad spirit. The greatest risk to the Church, he believes, is to accept the role contemporary Western secularism has assigned the Church — a private institution that should stay silent.

Parrhesia stems from the Pope's conviction that the Holy Spirit is in charge of the Church, and that his task is to allow it to course more freely by opening up new spaces — above all in spheres that are traditionally allergic to the Church. *Parrhesia* is about finding your voice, and using it — in the media studio, the office, the pub or coffee shop, among friends, and at those dinner parties that suddenly freeze over. We hope this book helps.

Catholic Voices Prayer

God our Father,
Bless and guide all those involved in Catholic Voices.
Give us the gifts of the Holy Spirit that we need for this work,
especially wisdom, gentleness, courage and joy.
Help us to be faithful to Christ and to his Church,
and to be open to the questions that people bring us.
Help us to love and respect all those we meet.
Support us in our difficulties and setbacks.
May our words and the witness of our lives
give you glory and help others to be more open to you.
We make this prayer through Christ our Lord. Amen.

Our Lady, Seat of Wisdom, pray for us.
Saints John XXIII and John Paul II, pray for us.
Blessed Titus Brandsma, pray for us.
Blessed Cardinal Newman, pray for us.

Chapter 1

Tense Twins: *The Church and Political Life*

Challenging Questions

- Why does the Church interfere in politics — shouldn't it just stick to religious matters?
- Why does it try to tell Catholics how to vote — and put pressure on Catholic politicians on questions such as abortion?
- If it is a Church, why does it act like a state?

The prevailing ethic of autonomy is intrinsically hostile to allowing religion a voice in public life because it sees religion as a private matter and public life as a neutral space. Neither is true, but both ideas are central to what might be called the founding myth of liberal states. In *Inventing the Individual: The Origins of Western Liberalism*, Oxford academic Larry Siedentop shows how it was the Christian conception of God underpinning medieval thought that gave rise to the respect for individual conscience, rights and autonomy that so characterise contemporary democracy. But having become detached from its origins in Christianity, modern liberalism now represents a radical individualism, one that resents community, religion and history, and blames all worldviews (apart from its own) as imperialistic anachronisms.

As a result, Catholics are told that the Church has no right to 'impose' its beliefs or to 'meddle' in politics. The Church stands accused of acting as a kind of lobby, using its spiritual influence to engineer certain political outcomes — acting, in other words, out of corporate self-interest. The criticism is accentuated by the Vatican's status as a state, and the way it uses its diplomatic network (as well as its observer status at the United Nations) to seek to influence global policy.

Those on the political left object to the way the Holy See opposes the bid to impose 'reproductive rights' — abortion and sterilisation programmes — on poor countries of the world, although the same critics tend not to object to its efforts to end the death penalty, broker peace, or persuade nations to curb carbon emissions. On the political right, conversely, there is little protest when the Holy See works to expand religious freedom across the world or to oppose what Pope Francis calls the "ideological colonisation" of same-sex marriage. Conservatives are much less happy, however, about the Holy See backing employment rights, critiquing market capitalism, or speaking up for the rights of migrants and refugees. In other words, when the Vatican is criticised for speaking out, it is usually because their position clashes with the critic's political prejudices.

Domestically, meanwhile, the Church is accused of interfering in the democratic process in a number of ways: by 'telling Catholics how to vote' at elections; by lobbying governments, bringing to bear its corporate influence on the Oireachtas; or by coercing Catholic politicians into voting according to the Church's dictates under threat of denying them Holy Communion.

What is — or should be — the Church's proper relationship with the state and politics? How, and with what justification, does it speak out on social, political, and economic questions? And what do Catholics stand for?

 POSITIVE INTENTION

Keeping separate the spheres of religion and politics is a Christian concept, with its origin in the temporal-spiritual distinctions of the Middle Ages. It is even more important in a pluralistic society, where the public sphere should be a place for rational discussion in which differing narratives of the good can interact and compete.

The Church should promote the common good, not its narrow self-interest, and it should contribute to public discussion not by an appeal to theological concepts but in the public language of rationality. Above all, the Church should not use the power of the state or of law to proselytise or coerce; truth persuades on its own merits, and the Church, as Pope Francis says, must grow by attracting, not proselytising. Another positive value fuelling the criticism is that the Church should stand for progress in human history, not seek to block it.

Religion and Politics — Tense Twins

What is the proper relationship between spiritual and temporal, religion and politics, Church and state? It's not that clear; and nor should it be. Democracy and public life are at their best when the two spheres are in constant tension, interacting. Turf wars between popes and emperors are the stuff of medieval history; nowadays, as we'll see in the next chapter, there is tension between the state's drive to create equality and the right to religious freedom. The tension is healthy. Countries with official policies that seek to insulate the state from religious influences — Mexico, China, and Cuba — are the poorer for it. Religion, in many forms, has an influence not just on private belief but public policy; it is much healthier to allow it to play its part in public, rational debate about matters of common concern.

It is common to hear that religion and politics should be kept apart. But what is meant by 'religion'? The contemporary meaning of the word 'religion' came into being along with the ideology underpinning modern Western democracies that seeks to separate private and public, religious and secular. In *The Myth of Religious Violence*, William T. Cavanaugh shows that the idea that 'religion' should have nothing to do with 'rational' spheres such as economics and politics is "one of the foundational legitimising myths of the liberal nation-state".

The claim rests on the myth that religion is somehow dangerous because it is absolutist or divisive, yet, Cavanaugh shows, "ideologies and institutions labelled secular can be just as absolutist, divisive, and irrational as those labelled religious". After the so-called Wars of Religion in Europe in the sixteenth and seventeenth centuries, the transference of 'the holy' from international Church to national state did not lead to the end of violence: the nation-state became a new kind of religion — which is why millions in the twentieth century died for the sake of their country, or an ideology. So-called secular ideologies such as nationalism, patriotism, liberalism, Marxism and capitalism have consistently produced behaviour that is absolutist, divisive, and violent.

Of course, religious people have been violent, and religion has played its fair share in wars. But before the modern era it was impossible to separate 'religion' from other institutional forces and factors that were also involved — tribal rivalry, political ambition, economic greed, etc. Only in the modern era has there been an attempt to create a category of 'religion' separate from 'secular,' but the terms are barely coherent.

Religio in ancient times meant not only worship, but also civic oaths and family rituals, which are now considered secular. The term comes from *re-ligare*, to bind together or re-link; it refers to social relations. In the Middle Ages, 'religious' was used to describe men and women in orders, who took vows and lived by a Rule, as opposed to 'secular' priests under a bishop. Religion was not a separate sphere of activity from politics, or from other 'secular' realms. But they were distinct spheres, reflecting differing functions between temporal and spiritual. This was not a theocracy: not every sin was a crime, nor every crime a sin; there were different courts and laws for clergy and laity. But all worked to the same end and shared the same religious view of life and activity.

With the dawn of modernity, however, 'religion' came to mean an essentially interior, private activity, distinct from pursuits such as politics and economics. The religious-secular binary was invented by those who wanted to declare the independence of one from the other, and is asserted above all today by those who see the function of the state as defending the individual and the public sphere from the incursion of religion. But this ideology makes little sense. Many politicians, for example, will describe their faith as part of their motivation for entering public life.

The attempt to drive religion out of politics does not have a happy history. The greatest horrors of the twentieth century were inflicted by totalitarian states among whose first moves was the abolition of faith from the public sphere and the subordination of religion to the state, justified by an ideology that interprets the 'will of the people' as a licence for unchecked, unlimited power. Among the first moves of communist and many fascist regimes was to abolish any legal recognition of God and to impose compulsory atheism classes; religion pointed to a power and authority beyond state control and therefore implied limits to the state.

Conversely, some of the proudest moments of Western political history — the abolition of the slave trade, for example, or the civil rights movement of the 1950s and 1960s — are uplifting examples of what happens when religion enters politics. The greatest achievements in Western history are products of a civilisation in which Church and state cooperate, and reason and faith are in dialogue. In Northern Ireland, when the atmosphere was too toxic to allow politicians to speak across the sectarian divide, courageous clergy and laity from different Christian denominations worked together on ecumenical programmes and began to build bridges which laid foundations for the peace process.

Religious freedom underpins democracy and pluralism. True democracy allows religion — on an equal basis, of course, with other creeds and worldviews — a voice in the public sphere. In the Christian tradition, the two spheres of faith and politics are distinct yet inter-connected. Unlike secularism, which proclaims the moral autonomy of the state (except from liberal ideology), a healthy or positive secularity advocates a distinction between faith and politics, not their divorce. The precise relationship of faith and politics, spiritual and temporal, is a complex one, and there are many different models in different Western countries. But the underlying principle should be clear. Neither fundamentalism (in which religious authorities take over the mechanism of the state) nor secularism (which declares the public sphere a religion-neutral zone) offers the right model. "Religious fundamentalism and secularism are alike in that both represent extreme forms of a rejection of legitimate pluralism and the principle of secularity," observed Pope Benedict in his January 1, 2011, World Peace Day message.

Reason and religion need each other; they are inextricably bound together. "Religious reasoning is a branch of human rationality," notes Roger Trigg in his book *Religion in Public Life*. "It has as much right to be heard as any form of scientific reasoning and is sometimes in as much need of critical scrutiny."

When critics resent the Church for 'interfering' or for 'playing politics,' it usually means they disagree with the Church's position rather than its decision to speak out. The same critic will usually say nothing when the Church has intervened politically on a matter with which they agree. Some accuse the Church of being reactionary or right-wing for opposing 'women's rights' (in arguing against abortion laws) or 'gay rights' (when it opposes, say, same-sex adoption), or of being left-wing in advocating a right to housing or an end to direct provision for asylum seekers, opposing the death penalty, or criticising a model of economic growth that puts money before people.

In short, people are against the Church 'interfering' in what they would much rather be left alone; and in favour of 'interfering' in what they believe should be changed. So, when should the Church speak out on political matters?

When to Speak and When to Stay Silent

When should the Church speak? The answer is rarely and cautiously, and almost always because it is a matter that touches on questions of human dignity, on core freedoms and rights (such as the right to life or to religious freedom), or on basic principles of Catholic social teaching, which is the fruit of the Church's ethical reflections on what makes for human flourishing. In these cases, the Church not only needs to speak out; it has a *duty* to do so.

When it speaks, the Church typically prefers to lay down broad ethical principles rather than attacking particular policies or parties, leaving those involved to argue about the application of the principles. The bishops might tell you, for example, that people have a right to a dignified standard of living, that persons who are unemployed deserve to be treated with respect. They will also say that the state has finite resources and people ought to be encouraged to play a fuller role in society by taking up employment if they can. What social welfare policy flows from these principles? Bishops might get involved in that question, but generally they leave it to politicians to debate and work out.

The Church promotes active citizenship and political engagement. Church leaders tell Catholics to get out and vote, and to be involved. Catholics are simultaneously members of the Church and citizens who obey the law and work for the good of the nation wherever they are, whatever regime they are under. This 'dual citizenship' is not a divided loyalty, for there is no contradiction, but it does produce a healthy tension. Living in the world while looking to a transcendent horizon is one reason why Catholics are unusually active in politics in countries where they are not a majority. In the United States, for example, about a third of members of Congress are Catholic, divided almost equally between Republicans and Democrats.

The Church typically doesn't tell Catholics who to vote for, but rather what they believe Catholics should be concerned about in any given election. The Church is not partisan; it does not favour one political party over another. Nor does it blow with the wind; it starts from deep-seated principles that stand true in spite of changing times. It is the bishops' task to articulate Catholic teaching on behalf of Catholic voters in the language of reason, and the voters' task to challenge candidates to respond to them; and then to decide, in conscience, how to vote.

In a modern democracy, the Church has a right to speak out for the same reason any other civil-society association or organisation does — a natural right to proclaim and promote its values, and to persuade others of these values; to get a debate going about the health of society and its priorities, applying the wisdom and insights of the Christian tradition to the great questions besetting contemporary society. The Church does this because it cares, above all, for the 'common good,' described by the *Catechism of the Catholic Church* as "the sum total of social conditions which allow people, either as groups or as individuals, to reach their fulfilment more fully and more easily". The common good is a key tenet of the Church's vision for society and the principles which it believes lie behind its healthy functioning.

The Church in Ireland can claim some influence over the 78.3% of citizens of the Republic who choose to self-identify as Catholics and the 45% of people in the North who self-identify as Catholics, but its right and duty to speak out isn't contingent on its numbers. Even where the Church is tiny — in certain Middle Eastern or Asian countries, for example — bishops still make their voice heard, trusting that the ethical principles they evoke will appeal to all people of goodwill. The Church seeks to persuade, not to impose; to attract, not to cajole. It does so, however, from a position of authority, as the most significant civil society actor on the world stage and as the guardian of the tradition which shaped the moral and cultural values of the Western world. And because it is politically and nationally independent, it can ask questions of society that others are not prepared to ask — and it is uniquely qualified, by its pastoral involvement in communities across the world, to speak for those deprived of a voice.

A Global Actor with a Global Perspective

The Church has about 1.28 billion adherents — 16.8% of the world's population — on all the continents. About half of that population is in the Americas and just under a quarter in Europe, while there are fast-growing populations in Africa (17%), Asia (11%) and Oceania (less than one percent). Across the world, in hundreds of countries, there are over 5,000 bishops, around 415,000 priests, 45,000 married deacons, 54,000 religious brothers and more than 670,000 religious sisters. The Church runs more than 220,000 parishes, 5,000 hospitals, 17,500 dispensaries and 15,000 homes for the elderly, along with tens of thousands of schools. It can claim to be one of the largest, if not the largest, aid and development body. Caritas Internationalis, the seventy-year old Rome-based confederation of 165 national bodies of Catholic charities in more than 200 countries, estimates their combined annual budget at over €4 billion. Trócaire, the Church in Ireland's overseas development agency, raised more than €22 million to help some of the world's poorest people. During their annual Lenten campaign in 2017 they distributed one million collection boxes to parishes that raised €7.4 million in just 40 days during the penitential season. In Africa — to take just one continent — the Church runs a quarter of all the hospitals, and its schools educate around 12 million children each year. The Catholic Church cares for, teaches, instructs, and is present in the lives of millions across the globe. It is the largest and most influential actor in global civil society.

The combined experience and wisdom of this presence is why the Church can speak as the world's leading moral teacher and guide — an 'expert in humanity,' as the Vatican's Justice and Peace Council puts it.

The Catholic Church is the only religious body to have an official presence — that of Observer Status — at the United Nations. It is the only religion with a diplomatic corps (the oldest still in existence). Worldwide, the Church is a crucial backer of the Sustainable Development Goals (SDGs), the UN's global action plan, and tireless promoter of debt cancellation and other forms of financial aid to developing countries. The Vatican is the world's first carbon-neutral state, setting an example that Pope Francis wants the Church worldwide to follow, putting good stewardship of creation in front and centre of its social concerns. The Holy See plays a crucial role in disarmament negotiations and arms trade treaties, in campaigning against the death penalty worldwide, in negotiating the release of hostages, and in conflict resolution. And it advocates reforms designed to place the economy more at the service of humanity. In 2011, for example, the Vatican's Justice and Peace Council called for new global structures capable of restraining and regulating the international financial markets for the sake of the common good, backing in particular the idea of a tax on financial transactions.

These might all be considered 'progressive' initiatives but the Church would also regard as progressive its opposition to abortion laws, assisted suicide, same-sex marriage, embryonic stem-cell research, in vitro fertilisation and maternal surrogacy, as well as its opposition to the death penalty and its advocacy of migrants, victims of human trafficking and the unemployed. What all these issues have in common is the defence of the dignity of the human person — even if that dignity is not recognised by wider society. The rights and dignity of the aborted unborn, children deprived of a mother and a father in a same-sex relationship, the elderly in hospitals, and the foreign-born are not recognised, says Pope Francis in a powerful metaphor, because they are victims of a 'throwaway culture': "Unfortunately, what is thrown away is not only food and dispensable objects," he says, "but often human beings themselves, who are discarded as unnecessary."

Because of its global presence and perspective, the Holy See is uniquely able to coordinate responses to global challenges such as human trafficking, the arms trade, and the death penalty. And because of its 2,000-year experience of reflecting on the state of the world in the light of the Gospel, it can offer diagnoses and cures that go to the heart of the issue — as Pope Francis did in his bracing encyclical on the environment, *Laudato Si'*.

It can also offer support to those who fall outside the traditional structures (such as trade unions) that protect vulnerable people. In October 2014, Pope Francis addressed a world meeting of 'popular movements' to call for their rights to be recognised. It is hard to imagine any other world leader telling waste-collectors, recyclers, peddlers, seamstresses, fishermen, farmworkers, and other workers in the informal sector that "from now on every worker, within the formal system of salaried employment or outside it, should have the right to decent remuneration, to social security, and to a pension...Today I want to join my voice to yours and support you in your struggle."

Vatican or Holy See?

Vatican City is a small (if magnificent) area in Rome recognised as a state as a result of the 1929 Lateran Pacts. These agreements, signed with the Italian dictator Benito Mussolini, brought to an end a long-running question concerning the Vatican's territorial sovereignty following the loss of the Papal States and Italy's birth as a nation-state in 1861.

It is sometimes claimed that the Vatican is only recognised internationally because of the Lateran Pacts. However, the Vatican's status as a state is different than the international sovereign jurisdiction of the Holy See, which has been recognised for centuries, long before 1929. Britain's oldest diplomatic relationship, for example, is with the Holy See — first established formally in 1479, and re-established in 1914, many years before the Lateran Pacts. The nascent Irish Free State established diplomatic relations with the Vatican in 1929. However, Cardinal Giovanni Battista Rinuccini was the first papal envoy sent to Ireland by Pope Innocent X in 1645 to help the confederate Catholics in their struggle against the English. The United States had consular relations with the Papal States starting in 1797 under President George Washington, but ties were interrupted in 1870 due in large part to national anti-Catholic sentiment. In 1984, President Ronald Reagan established diplomatic relations with the Holy See and named the first US ambassador to the Holy See.

The Lateran Pacts mean that the Vatican is an insignificant state in the hard-power sense of armies or economic muscle. But judged by its ability to move hearts and minds, it is a 'soft superpower'. Sometimes the results are spectacular, as with the role Pope St John Paul II played in the collapse of the Soviet empire. Other times, such as with the restoration of US-Cuba ties in December 2014 as a result of Pope Francis' patient mediation, they show how effective the Church's behind-the-scenes diplomatic network can be.

The Holy See is the seat of governance of the worldwide Catholic Church. It has international sovereign jurisdiction, meaning that it is recognised as a legal entity with which governments have relations. This sovereignty is what enables, for example, the bishop of a local diocese to be appointed by the Vatican rather than by the local government. It is also what gives the Church an important degree of independence from political power. Religious freedom — the freedom to worship, manifest one's belief, and so on — is safeguarded by the Catholic Church's independence, manifest in its international sovereignty.

Much of what the Holy See achieves worldwide — the result of bringing its moral authority and global presence to bear on countries to help effect change — is possible because of this sovereign international jurisdiction. The Holy See has had a continuous history as an organisation since the fourth century, which makes it older than most nation-states. And that relationship is not restricted to Catholic countries: 183 states have diplomatic relations with the Holy See, and more than 80 ambassadors to the Holy See are resident in Rome.

The résumé of the current secretary of state, Cardinal Pietro Parolin, gives an insight into the kind of diplomatic activity the Holy See engages in. He cemented ties between the Holy See and Vietnam, laying the foundations for religious freedom there, and effected a breakthrough in relations with China. He was at the forefront of Vatican efforts to approve the Nuclear Non-Proliferation Treaty and was responsible for freeing 15 British navy personnel captured by Iranian forces in the Arabian Gulf in April 2007. Later, as undersecretary, he was involved in mediating in trouble spots such as Timor-Leste and in brokering peace between Ecuador and Peru over disputed borders, as well as pushing international efforts to ban cluster bombs. Since his appointment, he has overseen the Vatican's efforts to combat human trafficking.

Pierre Morel, a former French ambassador to the Vatican, says its role is unique in world diplomacy. "It expresses the deep frustrations of the world's peoples and its appeals come from the suffering of communities on both sides."

The Church in Ireland

When the Church raises its voice in Irish domestic affairs, it does so by virtue of its moral authority, its independent sovereign jurisdiction, and its strong presence in Irish civil society. In the Republic, Catholicism is the religious affiliation of the overwhelming majority of citizens. North of the border, Catholicism is fast approaching 50% of the population. Catholics attend and run 1,360 parishes across the island that are often the focal point for the local community. Parishes respond to the needs of the community in ways as diverse as parent and toddler groups, day care for the elderly, hot meals for those experiencing homelessness, food banks for those in need and as hosts for organisations like Alcoholics Anonymous. In challenging communities, parishes and religious organisations have pioneered initiatives like breakfast clubs for children and after-school spaces where children can complete their homework in a calm and safe environment. Parishes run youth clubs and other activities to ensure that young people have somewhere to escape from hanging around on street corners at the lure of criminal gangs.

The Church is at the forefront of addressing pressing social needs like homelessness, poverty and alienation. Figures such as Fr Peter McVerry, Sr Stanislaus Kennedy, Bro. Kevin Crowley and Sr Consilio have become household names because of how they manifest the charity of Christ to some of Ireland's most vulnerable people in contemporary society. Diocesan social service agencies work to alleviate poverty and substance abuse in parishes and organisations like Accord and Cura counsel people who are experiencing relationship difficulties or a crisis pregnancy.

According to the European Social Survey, about a third of Irish Catholics attend Mass weekly. Estimates put the number at 150,000, demonstrating, by the standards of contemporary society, a highly unusual level of engagement and commitment. They show that commitment in countless other ways. Many of these people are actively involved in organisations such as the Society of St Vincent de Paul, the Legion of Mary, Trócaire and justice and peace groups. Many of the most vulnerable addicts who are denied places in state homelessness services as a result of their addiction have nowhere to turn to but religious-run hostels.

Practising Catholics, often motivated by their faith, also play a large role in voluntary organisations outside of a Church setting such as the Gaelic Athletic Association (GAA), tidy towns committees and local residents organisations. The Credit Union movement, which has helped countless people access credit they otherwise wouldn't have been able to, has its roots firmly in Catholic Social Teaching. In the United States, studies show that Catholics in every age group are more likely than the general population to volunteer.

The Catholic charitable sector in Ireland – North and South – is a massive contributor to the common good of the nation, conspicuous at the fringes of society, caring for those whom society has either left behind or scorns: the elderly, the disabled, children, young offenders, the homeless, asylum seekers, seafarers, persons with AIDS, prisoners, alcoholics, drug addicts, prostitutes, those who have been trafficked – the list is almost endless.

Catholics reach out to the poorest and most vulnerable irrespective of their beliefs. Catholic charitable action is not proselytising or trying to convert people: as Pope Benedict XVI wrote in *Deus Caritas Est*, "Those who practise charity in the Church's name will never seek to impose the Church's faith upon others." As many Catholics say, "We care for the poor not because *they* are Catholics but because *we* are." That doesn't make Catholic charitable action independent of faith; there is no greater witness to Christ's love than to serve the poor both through practical, direct assistance and through advocacy on their behalf. Before either can happen, the needs of the poor must first be 'sensed': Christianity has from its beginning been acutely tuned to human need. (Today's 'care industry,' which has grown out from the Church's networks of care, is too often detached from that primary 'sensing need'.)

The reality of Christian mission in today's parishes is a story of thousands of quiet kindnesses. In many of the most disadvantaged communities it is the Church and faith-based organisations that provide warmth, food, friendship and support for individuals who have fallen on the worst of times: the homeless, those in the grip of alcoholism or drug addiction, individuals with undiagnosed mental health problems, and those overwhelmed by multiple crises. They are all helped — in innumerable ways — by Christians. Churches provide debt counselling, English language lessons for migrants, emergency accommodation, and, sometimes most important of all, someone to listen. The energies and lives of most clergy and many Massgoers are taken up with helping others in practical ways — responding to their gratitude to Christ through service to others.

In 2016, the Society of St Vincent de Paul spent €35 million helping some 140,000 people across the country with vital needs such as food and fuel vouchers. Thousands of SVP volunteers spend their evenings and weekends visiting vulnerable people in their communities and helping out. In Dublin alone, Crosscare, the social care agency of the archdiocese, accommodated 2,024 people and 125 families experiencing homelessness in 2016. In the same year, Crosscare supported 4,726 young people through youth clubs and summer programmes, provided 127,720 hot meals to those in need ancd distributed 1,468 tonnes of donated food. In all, 1,850 Crosscare volunteers are working across the Dublin Archdiocese with vulnerable communities and individuals. Every Christmas Day in Dublin, the Knights of Columbanus – a Catholic lay organisation – transform the RDS into a festive venue and serve a Christmas lunch to hundreds of people with nowhere else to go.

Catholic charities often do what no one else does, blazing a trail others later follow — out on the edge with those on the edge. There are countless examples of charitable outreach pioneered by Catholics that over time became 'mainstream' charitable activities; hospices caring for the terminally ill are a prime example. Others remain preserves of the Church. No organisation compares with the Apostleship of the Sea, which provides support and assistance to hundreds of thousands of seafarers visiting ports each year.

Although ultimately inspired by the Gospel, most of these charities are directly motivated by the example of a charismatic founder, often a saint. They grow directly out of civil society (rather than as a creation of the state), and frequently depend on and work through parishes and schools, galvanising the energies and passions of networks of volunteers.

Finally, Catholics are guided by a coherent set of principles, embodied in Catholic social teaching, which in turn enrich Irish social and political thinking and strengthen civil society. Through nationwide organisations, Catholic charities advocate on behalf of those they serve, influencing policy decisions and helping to shape laws that serve the interests of the poor.

Irish Catholics also make a massive contribution to overseas development and humanitarian relief through the bishops' agency Trócaire. Founded in 1973 to coordinate development and emergency relief, Trócaire now works with local and Church partners to support communities in over 20 developing countries with a focus on food and resource rights, women's empowerment and humanitarian response. Working with hundreds of active partners worldwide — usually the local Church — Trócaire tackles international poverty. It also works to influence global decisions through its membership in the Vatican-based Caritas Internationalis.

The Irish Bishops' Conference – headquartered at Maynooth – works to develop links between the Church and legislators and officials. Those links not only help relations between Church and state, but also provide a much-needed channel of communication between civil society and government. Because the Church is present among the poorest and most vulnerable in society, it can be their voice in the corridors of power, calling for a living wage and focusing public attention on joblessness and poverty.

Bishops, Elections, Politicians, and Conscience

Critics of this arrangement make the claim that the Church seeks to 'impose its view' through the use of a kind of moral coercion, interfering in the democratic process. A favourite example: bishops refusing to give Holy Communion to politicians who fail to 'toe the line'.

But this is to look at it the wrong way. When vital Church teaching is being misrepresented by public officials in such a way as to risk misleading the faithful, bishops are obligated to take action to clarify the issue.

This has arisen specifically in the case of abortion because it is concerned with the sanctity of life, which the Church believes should be reflected in society's rule of law by defending the basic right to life from conception to natural death. In order for a Catholic to be in full communion with the faith of the Church, he or she must accept this teaching. Referring to laws that promote or authorise abortion and euthanasia, Pope St John Paul II's encyclical letter *Evangelium Vitae* notes "a grave and clear obligation to oppose them by conscientious objection" (no. 73).

Cardinal Joseph Ratzinger (who later became Pope Benedict XVI) in 2004 advised US bishops to speak privately with prominent Catholics who defy Church teachings on key issues involving the sanctity of life, alert them to the gravity of their offences, and warn them that they will be refused Holy Communion if they do not change their ways. Only if these warnings are not heeded, Cardinal Ratzinger added, "and the person in question, with obstinate persistence, still presents himself to receive the Holy Eucharist, the minister of Holy Communion must refuse to distribute it."

The issue for the US bishops that election year was not how to influence the outcome. It was rather how to deal with the scandal arising from a public Catholic who was publicly violating Church teaching in an essential matter of ethics, without it looking as if the bishops were weighing into party politics. Cardinal Ratzinger's solution reflected this concern; he advocated the public barring from Communion only as a matter of last resort. The Church upholds as an important first principle that political battles should be fought, in the words of the Archbishop of Washington at the time, Cardinal Theodore McCarrick, "not at the Communion rail but in the public sphere, in hearts and minds, in our pulpits and public advocacy, in our consciences and communities."

What the Church Stands For

When Catholics vote or become politically active, their priorities and concerns will differ, along with their loyalties and their affiliations. But there are key principles on which all Catholics should agree because they have been consistently taught by the Church since 1891 when Pope Leo XIII issued the first 'social encyclical' of modern times: *Rerum Novarum*. Since then, there have been many more encyclicals — the latest are Pope Benedict XVI's 2007 *Caritas in Veritate* and Pope Francis' 2015 *Laudato Si'* — along with many other Church documents expanding on and applying these principles to contemporary challenges.

These principles are captured in a body of teaching known as Catholic Social Teaching (CST). It offers a set of principles for reflection, criteria for judgment, and directives for action. Its purpose is to contribute to the formation of conscience as a basis for specific action. It amounts, in effect, to a Catholic vision of politics, society, and the economy.

In 2016, ahead of the general election in the Republic, the Irish bishops' conference issued a pastoral statement in which they insisted than an election "is an important moment which offers a democratic society an opportunity to reflect on its successes and failures". The bishops said that "democracy requires in the first place that all citizens exercise their right to vote and we strongly encourage all to vote in the upcoming election". The bishops also stressed that democracy is not limited to voting:

> "Democracy is fundamentally about people working and walking together to foster the common good. Democracy is damaged by indifference and by a splintering of society or a fixation on individual interests. A general election is a moment in which all citizens, and not just political parties, should reflect and take stock of the health of the nation and especially on how we respond to the plight of the most vulnerable.

Democracy flourishes when it is rooted in a shared social ethic. To succeed, good social policy requires economic stability and sustained growth. But economic growth on its own does not necessarily generate social equity. Social equity has a logic of its own which must be worked on to achieve its aim. Our comparatively wealthy Ireland has still a long path to travel in this task."

The bishops went on to highlight a number of key issues that they encouraged voters to talk to candidates about.

⌘ ***Health:*** most people feel great unease about the current health care system. They worry about what would happen to them if they became ill. They worry about the health of their children. They worry about what would happen to their parents and other elderly people should they become ill. They are worried about the cost of healthcare. They are worried about the quality of healthcare, including mental healthcare. Successive governments have presented a variety of solutions and in so many cases they have either failed or have not been implemented. A blame game is not the answer. Ireland's health crisis is the result of a fundamental failure of politics.

⌘ ***Home:*** there is a crisis of homelessness, not just of those who sleep rough on our streets, but of those who are housed in inadequate and precarious accommodation especially in hotel rooms totally unsuitable for children and families. All recognise that providing adequate and affordable social housing is an essential pillar of any solution. Some more recent social housing has been poor in quality. Private rental accommodation is scarce and property market dealings are even reducing the available pool.

⌘ ***Education:*** this general election takes place on the anniversary of the 1916 Rising and the Proclamation of a Republic which set out to cherish all the children of the nation equally. There has been much discussion about inequality in access to education. We are a young country and we will urgently need more and more new schools for the future. The real inequality in Irish schools is not religious in nature but it is the economic inequality where poorer communities and schools with a large percentage of disadvantaged children are not being adequately supported. Ireland is still marred by neglect of children and of lack of opportunity for the children of the most deprived and groups such as Travellers.

⌘ ***Security:*** citizens can only exercise their rights fully if they live within an overall climate of security. The most fundamental obligation of the state is the protection of its citizens. Recent killings on the streets of Ireland have shocked all of us. These are not simply about gangland feuds; they are the product of a criminal industry of death which unscrupulously floods our streets and our children with drugs. It is an 'industry' which destroys young lives daily and which fosters even broader criminality. People feel insecure in their homes both in rural and urban communities. They will willingly support policies which will strengthen An Garda Síochána.

⌘ ***Human ecology:*** Pope Francis speaks often of climate change. But he also speaks of a 'human ecology'. Austerity is not a popular word but there is another kind of austerity, that of simplicity in lifestyle in harmony with nature, through which all of us indicate where our real values lie, rather than in the empty values of consumerism and a rush for the superfluous. Families deserve much greater support in their work in fostering and transmitting values. A true human ecology recognises the equal right to life of every person from the moment of conception to the moment of natural death. The Constitution of Ireland embraces the right to life of the unborn child. It is a fundamental affirmation of equality, where the right to life of one child is not considered of less value than that of another. We strongly oppose any weakening of the affirmation of the right to life of the unborn.

⌘ ***International responsibility:*** Ireland is an island nation but not an isle of isolation. We belong within a global community. Ireland's missionary past is a clear indication of the deep concern of the people of Ireland for the progress of peoples worldwide. As a traditionally emigrant country we share a historical memory of how our emigrants were received or at times rejected in the lands to which they moved. Now is the time for us to reciprocate the experience of openness by welcoming to our communities people who flee from persecution, from economic exclusion or from religious discrimination. Despite economic challenges, Ireland can and must maintain its commitments in international life, especially recent commitments to finance development and to combat climate change.

In 2007, the United States Conference of Catholic Bishops issued a landmark document entitled *Forming Consciences for Faithful Citizenship*. In that document, the US bishops identify seven key themes of Catholic social teaching, or CST:

1. "The dignity of the human person is the foundation of a moral vision for society."

2. "The family — based on marriage between a man and a woman — is the first and fundamental unit of society and is a sanctuary for the creation and nurturing of children."

3. "Human dignity is respected and the common good is fostered only if human rights are protected and basic responsibilities are met."

4. "While the common good embraces all, those who are weak, vulnerable, and most in need deserve preferential concern. A basic moral test for our society is how we treat the most vulnerable in our midst."

5. "The economy must serve people, not the other way around."

6. "We are one human family, whatever our national, racial, ethnic, economic, and ideological differences. We are our brothers' and sisters' keepers, wherever they may be."

7. "Care for the earth is a duty of our faith and a sign of our concern for all people."

CST, which came into being in response to the development of modern Western capitalism, has two major concerns. The first is the alienation between capital and labour — the division of society into those who, on one side, control wealth and property, and the majority who, on the other, have to sell their labour. (It was the growth of the poverty-stricken masses in the cities of Europe that sparked Pope Leo's encyclical.) The second is the growth in power of the market and the state, and the reduction in the size and the strength of civil society.

Put positively, the popes in seventeen key social encyclicals since 1891 have urged two essential reforms to the modern market polity and economy. The first is the 'humanisation' of the market, putting people before profits and remembering the human purpose of the economy. The second is a call for a strengthened civil society made up of vigorous 'intermediate associations', as opposed to a society seen as made up only of the state, capital, and isolated individuals.

CST has a number of key principles set out in a series of papal encyclicals and other Church documents over time: dignity of the human person, the common good, just wage, the universal destination of goods, solidarity, subsidiarity, participation, option for the poor, peace and disarmament, the preservation of life and creation and the call to action. Each of these themes is a rich mine of insight and wisdom into the right ordering of a modern, democratic, pluralistic society.

▣ EXISTING FRAME

The Catholic Church uses its power and influence to advance a reactionary agenda designed to frustrate progress in human rights and liberties. Bishops tell people how to vote and threaten politicians with excommunication when they don't do the Pope's bidding. The Church is essentially right-wing, seeking to impose outdated views on a secular state and on people who have no Christian allegiance.

↻ REFRAME

The Church raises its voice in the public sphere whenever an issue touches on the common good, often on questions of basic freedoms and rights, and especially when it can be a voice for the voiceless. Its authority to speak out derives from its moral authority and independence as one of the world's leading and oldest civil society organisations. It is neither right- nor left-wing, and has no allegiance to particular political parties, but exists to defend the common good and the Gospel in its integrity. It defends, and speaks up for, a distinction between the political and the religious; it upholds what it calls a 'positive secularity,' and deplores both religious fundamentalism and an aggressive kind of secularism that seeks to banish faith from the public sphere. The Catholic Church's political agenda can be summed up as Catholic social teaching plus religious freedom, the freedom that underpins all other rights and freedoms.

★ KEY MESSAGES

- The Church has a natural right to speak out derived from its moral authority and its presence in society.

- The Church advocates religious freedom and the proper distinction between faith and politics. At the same time, it calls for the political and the religious to be in dialogue, not separated.

- Bishops do not speak out before elections to persuade Catholics to vote one way or another; they identify the issues they think Catholics should be concerned about and that voters should be asking the candidates to address. Nor do they put pressure on politicians to vote this or that way by refusing them Communion.

- The Catholic Church's political agenda can be summed up in Catholic social teaching and religious freedom. It is an agenda that is the bedrock of freedom and civilisation, and is a key contribution in contemporary Western society to creating a society of human flourishing that recognises the God-given rights and the dignity of all people.

Chapter 2

Freedom and Equality: *Partners, Not Rivals*

- Why should the Church be allowed to discriminate against people when the law forbids it?
- If Catholic agencies don't want to obey the law, why should they then have access to public funds?
- Why should the Church be allowed to impose its dogmatic view of the family through taxpayer-funded services?
- Why should a business owner have the right to choose whom to serve based on his bigoted beliefs?

Ask people what they understand by 'religious freedom' and most will say that it means being allowed to believe in God, to convert from one faith to another, and to worship according to that faith without being coerced or harassed. Some will go further, and speak of the freedom to manifest belief: to organise and run institutions — schools, charities, and hospitals, institutes, and foundations — according to the principles of those beliefs. It quickly becomes apparent that religious freedom is not just about freedom for religious people; it is the basic liberty — along with the right to life — underpinning a civilised society. It is interesting to note that in framing the Proclamation of the Republic, the leaders of the 1916 Easter Rising put religious freedom as the first of the rights guaranteed to citizens in the new state. For many of those who took part in 1916 and the subsequent War of Independence, the freedom to be Catholic was central to how they viewed their struggle for freedom. Religious freedom should be understood, as Pope Benedict XVI put it in January 2011, not as immunity from coercion, "but even more fundamentally as an ability to order one's own choices in accordance with truth". As Pope Francis said in June 2014:

"Reason recognises in religious freedom a fundamental human right that reflects the highest human dignity, the ability to seek the truth and conform to it, and recognises in it a condition that is indispensable to the ability to deploy all of one's own potentiality. Religious freedom is not only that of private thought or worship. It is the liberty to live, both privately and publicly, according to the ethical principles resulting from found truth. This is a great challenge in the globalised world, where weak thought — which is like a disease — also lowers the general ethical level, and in the name of a false concept of tolerance, it ends in persecuting those who defend the truth about man and its ethical consequences."

Religious freedom enters contemporary news reports and debates in two ways. The first is the epidemic of persecution and suppression of religious belief and practice across the world, directed especially at the Church: 80% of acts of religious intolerance today, according to the International Society for Human Rights, a secular body based in Frankfurt, are against Christians. "The most dramatic Christian story of our time," says US journalist John Allen, "is that there is a completely non-metaphorical war on religion, and on Christianity, afoot in a growing number of places in the world." Yet because in the liberal frame the Church is seen as having a hegemonic role — creating victims — the story is largely ignored in the Western media, which struggle to see Christians as a persecuted minority. As Pope Francis commented following a massacre of Catholics and Anglicans in Lahore, Pakistan, in March 2015, this is a persecution "that the world seeks to hide".

The other religious freedom story is in the West, which is often ignored for a different reason: because *religious freedom* is assumed in the ethics of autonomy to be *freedom of worship* — a private affair, with no relevance to the public sphere — and who in the West doesn't have that? So, when the principle of religious freedom is invoked, the assumption is often that it is a way of justifying some other agenda, such as an attack on the rights of minorities. That may happen in some cases. But when the Church invokes the principle, it is because governments driven by the ethics of autonomy are seeking to build law and culture around a concept of religion as a private matter, and therefore making it hard for believers to manifest their belief in the public sphere.

The clashes are taking place above all as the state — under the banner of equality and civil rights — adopts positions that reflect new ideologies of gender and sexuality and demand that civil-society institutions conform to its positions. In the United States, the clash has been particularly intense over the so-called HHS mandate, a national health-care law mandating that employers — including a whole host of religious charities, schools, hospitals, and other faith-based non-profits — provide health-care insurance that includes abortion-inducing drugs, contraception and female sterilisation. The law aims to coerce those who run these services into acting contrary to their consciences.

In making their case against the HHS mandate, the Catholic Church and the US Catholic bishops have been accused of being stuck in the past, against civil rights, and waging a war on women. The frame is tragically misleading. The Church is the leading advocate for the marginalised and the vulnerable, an enemy of unjust discrimination, and a pioneer of American health care and education, driven above all by American Catholic women serving the poorest in society.

Inflaming these debates is an assumption that equality and religious freedom are rivals, in which Catholics who stand up for faith are accused of being 'opposed to equality', of 'seeking the right to discriminate', and failing to grasp a basic tenet of liberal democracy, namely the equality of every individual before the law. Advocates of the HHS mandate see it as giving women an equal right to access health care, and accuse the Church of seeking to 'impose' its view on them. The battles have been heated and intense. As Cardinal Timothy Dolan of New York told NBC's *Meet the Press* in April 2015: "We've got to make sure that the rights of conscience and religious ability to publicly exercise one's religion is balanced with another good, namely the rights of people not to be discriminated against."

✝ POSITIVE INTENTION

Advocates of equality start from a position enshrined in human rights doctrine that has its origins in the idea that all people share the same Creator and have equal dignity and worth. In a modern plural democracy, all should be equal before the law and their rights respected, regardless of race, religion, gender, sexual orientation, or disability. The historic Gospel task of emancipating those who have been marginalised and excluded from society is evident today in many of our laws: a wheelchair user should in principle have the same access as an able-bodied person to public buildings; a woman cannot be dismissed from her job simply because she is pregnant; a Protestant candidate should not be preferred to a Catholic candidate during a job interview simply on the grounds of religion.

Equality and the State

The equalities ideal is rooted in the basic Christian principle that all are equal in worth and dignity before God. Yet 'equality' is not a fixed value — something people either believe in or not, accept or not — but a strongly contested notion involving questions of values and rights. As Aristotle said, "The worst form of inequality is to try to make unequal things equal." The law can and does discriminate with good reason; equality should not flatten valid distinctions. At the same time, equality does not mean applying the law equally to everyone; for the sake of justice, it is necessary sometimes to exempt some groups from the application of the law — or apply the law in some areas but not in others.

A 'just' or 'legitimate' discrimination is when the law refuses to recognise an equal right for good reasons. Thus, the law prohibits racially-segregated public toilets, but not public toilets segregated by gender. In the first case, the motivation for the exclusion is irrational prejudice; in the second the motive is the recognition of legitimately differing needs and rights. The first is discriminatory, but not the second. The Church refers to the first as *unjust* discrimination — something it is firmly against.

Why urge legal equality? Not to make everyone and everything the same, but to remove unjust barriers to participation in society, democracy, and economy when those barriers are based on irrational prejudice or unfair criteria. Discrimination occurs when things or people that should be treated in the same way by the law are treated less favourably. But when that differential is reasonable or just, it is not (unjust) discrimination.

The state discriminates when it offers certain benefits to the elderly, or to those who are married; if those same benefits were extended to everyone, the state would no longer be offering special protection to pensioners or supporting marriage. A pension that is available to people younger than 65 ceases to be a pension, just as (see Chapter 5) a marriage that is made available to a same-sex couple ceases to be a marriage as traditionally understood. As Archbishop Salvatore Cordileone of San Francisco put it, speaking of same-sex marriage, "We recognise and respect the equal human dignity of everyone. Everyone should be treated equally, but it is not discrimination to treat differently things that are different. Marriage really is unique for a reason."

Another area is the implementation of equality laws. Giving 'equality' to one group in society can seriously prejudice the rights and interests of another group. The general principle of curbing unjust discrimination — no one should be allowed in law to refuse to employ or offer a service to someone on the grounds of race, gender, or disability — is one shared by the Church. The disagreements arise over *how* those equality laws are implemented. And behind that disagreement are different perceptions of state and society.

When laws are proposed or enacted that directly affect a community's 'natural' freedoms and rights, or that seek to coerce them in a way that violates their conscience, there are various rights and goods at play. The key principle to democracy is that the law should be applied wherever possible in such a way that accommodates minorities.

Military conscientious objection is a classic example of the respect the law pays to conscience. Another is the long tradition of allowing court witnesses who are non-Christian, or object to oath taking, to instead make a solemn 'affirmation' without putting a hand on the Bible. In more recent decades, 'conscience clauses' protect doctors, pharmacists and other health professionals from providing services or drugs to which they object as a matter of conscience.

Catholics strongly disagreed with the passage of the law permitting abortion in Britain in 1967, and they have continued to argue against it. The law respects that conscience-driven disagreement, so laws and regulations prohibit hospitals and other institutions receiving public funds from requiring doctors and nurses to participate in abortions.

The law, in other words, balances the position that a woman is free by law to choose an abortion with the recognition that a Catholic is free in conscience not to have to carry one out. The law is the law; and all are equal before it. But it is applied differently to different groups, where there is an important principle at stake. In a similar fashion, there is a provision in Irish law that provides that a faith-based school has a derogation from equality legislation to ensure that the school can protect its ethos by not being legally forced to employ a teacher who would undermine that same ethos. This pluralism is key to the equalities project. Sometimes communities need to be protected from the injurious effect of a law. They are not being allowed to 'opt out' of the law. They remain fully subject to the law, but the law in this instance treats them differently, noting that they have good reasons for being exempt. Allowing such exemptions is crucial to a healthy coexistence in a pluralistic society. It is also key to a democracy underpinned by religious freedom, one that allows the freedom of one faith alongside the freedom of other faiths or secular beliefs.

The implication of the HHS mandate in the US is that the Church's positions on abortion and contraception are born of irrational prejudice. The same idea lies behind regulations forcing Catholic adoption agencies in Britain to offer children to same-sex couples. The law is being used to coerce the Church into altering its teaching, in much the same way the law might be used to coerce people into renouncing racist or anti-social behaviour.

Yet to refuse a same-sex couple the right to adopt is not irrational prejudice; it arises from a deep-seated conviction about the nature of the family, which has long been the bedrock of human society, and the needs of the child to have a father and mother. So, too, with abortion, which the Church sees clearly as an unjust killing of innocent life, or contraception, which it sees as undermining the proper place of sex. Many Irish people might disagree with some or all of these beliefs, but is the state now declaring that it is 'irrational prejudice' to hold them?

Church and governments sometimes disagree over equality laws, in short, not because they disagree over the principle of equality understood as overcoming unjust discrimination, but over two models of state and society. The Church's model has the stronger liberal credentials, reflecting a deeper, richer pluralism, as opposed to a narrower, individualist model driven by the ethics of autonomy that seeks to privatise faith and diminish the freedom of religion.

The Freedom to Manifest Religion

Modern Western democracies separate Church and state and do not seek to impose religious beliefs on people, as happens in theocracies. But nor should they be 'secular theocracies', coercing Christians into acting against their consciences by imposing secular ideologies contrary to those convictions. As a rule, the state should reflect the variety of beliefs in society and seek to enact laws that are sensitive to the needs and rights of those diverse groups.

This is what Pope Benedict XVI referred to as a "positive secularity" — a religiously and ideologically neutral state that nevertheless respects and understands the needs and rights of faith. What the Church objects to as undemocratic is what Pope Benedict XVI called "aggressive secularism", in which the state fails to recognise the natural freedoms and rights of the Church in the public sphere, reducing religion to a merely private matter in which the Church is treated as an association of like-minded individuals rather than, as should be the case, a 'natural society' with its intrinsic freedoms and rights. Then Taoiseach Bertie Ahern summed up his feelings on the issue in a 2008 speech on the important role of faith groups in society. He described as "worrying" the trend to "attempt to exclude matters of faith and religious belief from public debate and confine them to the purely personal, with no social or public significance...It is, I believe, fundamentally illiberal and anti-democratic to silence opinions and views, and marginalise institutions and communities which draw their identity and ethical positions from a background of religious belief".

What Catholics object to is not a religiously-neutral state that treats the Church on a par with other beliefs and worldviews; the Church calls precisely for that in the Second Vatican Council's declaration on religious freedom, *Dignitatis Humanae*. What it objects to is the imposition of an ideology, driven by ethics of autonomy, that fails to recognise the freedom of religion, understood in its full sense as freedom to manifest religion.

A key principle of religious liberty is that charities and schools and other civil society bodies should be free to 'manifest belief,' namely, to create organisations inspired by and witnessing to their religious ethos. That means selecting certain kinds of people to run them, and having policies and practices that witness to the values underpinning them. Faith-based organisations must be free to be consistent with their beliefs by the way they act — as long as they do not offend public order or inhibit the rights and freedoms of others. This freedom is much larger and more contentious than the 'freedom of worship'. It is also vital to civil society, which is nurtured and sustained by such value-driven organisations and persons.

The freedom to manifest belief includes the right to express or practice beliefs outside a place of worship as well as inside it. Providing health, charity, and education services, for example, are important ways Christians live out their faith. It also entails the right of faith communities to set their own rules for qualifications for religious office and for serving in religious institutions. Thus, reserving the priesthood to celibate men is not a violation of employment rules preventing discrimination against women and married men because the law respects the right of the Church to decide who qualifies for priesthood. As the United Nations Declaration on Religious Discrimination notes, "Religious tolerance includes respecting differences of opinions in these matters and respecting the difference between a state and a religious institution."

According to Cardinal George Pell, former Archbishop of Sydney, there are four main principles underpinning religious freedom:

1. Freedom of religion is not just the right to pray and believe, but to act on your beliefs in the public sphere, without being coerced or bullied by equality laws or claims that the beliefs are 'offensive'.

2. Freedom of religion means being free to provide services that are consistent with the beliefs of the sponsoring religion. The government has no right to say to religious agencies, "We like your work with vulnerable women; we just need you to offer them abortions as well," or, "We really like your schools, but we can't allow you to teach that marriage between a man and a woman is better or truer than other expressions of love and sexuality".

3. Religious freedom means being able to employ at least a critical mass of employees who support the ethos of the sponsoring religion. People who work in Catholic hospitals, schools, universities, welfare agencies, services for the refugees, the disabled, and the homeless do not all need to share the Catholic faith, but they need

to be happy to support it and work within it. It is also essential that a preference can be exercised for people who are actively committed to the religious convictions at the heart of these services.

4. Religious freedom means religious organisations should be able to receive public funding. The secular state is religiously neutral and has no mandate to exclude religion, especially when a large majority of the population are Christians or followers of other major religions. Church members also pay taxes. Substantial levels of government funding are no reason to prohibit religious schools, hospitals, and welfare agencies from offering services compatible with their beliefs, and provides no sufficient reason to coerce these entities to act against their principles.

In protesting against moves to restrict religious freedom, the Church has been defending not just its own freedom but the religious liberties of all, including business owners who want to run their businesses in accord with their religious values. This freedom of not only religious institutions but also people who happen to be religious in the public sphere is becoming more contested as the state seeks to coerce charities, social services and businesses into accepting an 'official' view of such questions. Some of the anger against the Church, especially from gay 'rights' activists and established feminists who see the Church as the enemy of their goals, betrays what Catholic Voices USA in a 2014 report to the United Nations called an "insatiable new intolerance".

> "Under this new intolerance, some Christian men and women now fear for their standing in the public sphere. Under this new intolerance, some also worry about the marginalising and stigmatising of their children. And in the face of pressure to act in lockstep with the ever-changing *desiderata* proclaimed by this new intolerance, some Christians also fear for their livelihoods as discrimination against people of faith creeps upward."

That this is happening in some of the very countries that have been known as beacons of tolerance is "an irony of enormous historical proportion," as the report put it. This new thinking "does not only seek the diminution of the Christian moral code. It also comes with — indeed, it ruthlessly insists upon — an alternative moral code of its own." The consequence of this new intolerance is to expand the sphere of the state and shrink that of civil society. Take the example of the Belfast-based firm Ashers Bakery, which was found guilty of discrimination for refusing to bake a cake with a political slogan promoting same-sex marriage. Even though the Christian McArthur family who run the firm were able to demonstrate to the courts that they did not even know the would-be customer's sexual orientation, the judges ruled that the refusal to ice the cake with the slogan was a breach of equality legislation and the firm had no right to refuse to bake cakes containing political slogans that contradicted their values.

The Civil-Society Principle

Religious freedom is not a small matter for the Church — or for society as a whole. As one of the leading actors in civil society — as we saw in Chapter 1 — it understands the importance of religious motivation. People set up, work for and give their lives to Church organisations because their faith inspires them. Feeling grateful for the gifts of God, being people of compassion and sensitive to the needs of the world, inspired by a strong sense of social justice and civic commitment, they establish schools, homeless shelters, child welfare charities, adoption agencies, hospices and countless other projects and institutes tackling addiction, family breakdown and poverty in all its forms.

These Catholic organisations do not limit their services to other Catholics; they serve the whole of society, addressing the needs of people regardless of their beliefs or backgrounds. The result is that Catholic civil organisations make a massive contribution to the common good of Ireland, worth many tens of millions of euros.

That is why the 'freedom to manifest belief' is so essential to a healthy civil society. Without the freedom to witness to the values of the Gospel and the teachings of the Catholic Church — what is usually described as 'Catholic ethos' — these organisations would shrivel and die or become empty shells, to the detriment of all. You can't have the fruits without the roots. For example, when the state threatens to remove public funding from Catholic marriage counselling services that are not open to counselling same-sex couples, the state runs the risk of dramatically undermining the common good by putting such vital services out of business and thus affecting couples in need of marriage guidance.

A healthy civil society produces good citizens. Democracy presupposes virtuous citizens but cannot produce them by itself. For the sake of democracy, government needs to support the authority, integrity and autonomy of civil society institutions, above all the family and the Church, which are nourished by the freedom to manifest belief. When equality laws restrict that freedom, it is democracy that suffers.

Religious freedom, in other words, is the civil-society principle. Where it is respected, civil society flourishes; where it is restricted, it has a chilling effect on civil society.

In his classic study of the breakdown of social capital, *Bowling Alone: The Collapse and Revival of American Community*, Harvard sociologist Robert D. Putnam showed how civic engagement and civic virtue were closely linked to relationships of trust, and that religion was the primary creator of those relationships. Religious people, he showed, make better neighbours and citizens, are more likely to give to charity, volunteer, assist a homeless person, donate blood, spend time with someone feeling depressed, offer a seat to a stranger, help someone find a job, and take part in local civic life. Affiliation with a religious community is the best predictor of altruism and empathy — better than education, age, income, gender or race.

The freedom to associate, believe, and then act on that belief is what makes a vigorous society possible.

Behind the refusal to grant exemptions for Catholic charities is the idea that the state acts on society in order to condition it — to impose a certain ideological view, in this case of the family. It also implies a model of society in which there is no such thing as 'intermediate associations', only individuals, families and the state. In the traditional Christian understanding, however, people belong not just to families but also have other, wider allegiances — to communities of value with different moral narratives. A nation, in this vision, is a 'community of communities'. It is the state's task to regulate the relationships between these communities, to prevent them from accumulating powers that prevent other communities from flourishing; it is not the state's task to impose an ideological narrative.

But in the individualist conception of state and society, there is nothing but a state and many individuals; therefore, one moral narrative must prevail. As Archbishop Charles Chaput of Philadelphia put it in 2013, critics of religious faith tend to reduce all moral convictions to an expression of subjective beliefs. "And if they're purely subjective beliefs, then — so the critics argue — they can't be rationally defended. And because they're rationally indefensible, they should be treated as a form of prejudice. In effect, two thousand years of moral experience, moral reasoning, and religious conviction become a species of bias."

In the case of adoption agencies, government is telling the Church that its organisations must accept the principle that same-sex couples are equal to the traditional family, and that this principle trumps their freedom to continue to advocate otherwise. This is what Pope Benedict memorably called the 'dictatorship of relativism'. "No one is forced to be a Christian," he told Peter Seewald in 2010. "But no one should be forced to live according to the 'new religion' as though it alone were definitive and obligatory for all mankind."

It is not the state's task to condition the consciences of its people, but rather to regulate and balance different rights and freedoms. This argument is not about the freedom of religious organisations to 'discriminate', but whether the state can be allowed to interfere with religious organisations and to impose on them relativist ideologies.

It is wrong, in principle, for anyone in a same-sex union to be denied a job simply on the grounds of that orientation, where that orientation is not remotely relevant to the job — as an accountant, for example. But if that person applies to be the principal of a Catholic school, it is relevant, because the Church teaches that sex is for marriage, which can only be between one man and one woman, and the principal of a Catholic school is responsible for witnessing to, and upholding, the ethos of the school. An anti-discrimination law that made it illegal for a school to 'discriminate' in this way would quickly undermine its ethos, and therefore its reason for existing.

Pretty soon there wouldn't be Catholic schools left, only schools that conformed to official ideology. And it wouldn't just be the Catholic charitable sector that shrank; civil society would all but disappear, leaving individuals naked before an almighty state.

The Irish Constitution, Bunreacht na hÉireann, is explicit in enshrining not only the right to worship but the right of the Church and other religious traditions to run themselves according to their own rules. Article 44.2.5 states that "every religious denomination shall have the right to manage its own affairs, own, acquire and administer property, movable and immovable, and maintain institutions for religious or charitable purposes." The Constitution also enshrines the principle that the State provides *for* education rather than providing education per se. Article 42 acknowledges that: "the primary and natural educator of the child is the family and guarantees to respect the inalienable right and duty of parents to provide, according to their means, for the religious and moral, intellectual, physical and social education of their children." The fact that the State funds Catholic schools, as well as other religious and non-religious schools, is an acknowledgement that it is parents rather than the State who choose how their children ought to be educated.

In recent years, the issue of the so-called 'baptism barrier' has entered the public discourse when it comes to education in the Republic. In a small number of cases, the local Catholic school has had to turn away children because the Government has not provided extra school places to meet an increase in population and the local school is over-subscribed. While the issue receives extensive media coverage, it is worth pointing out that research carried out by *The Irish Catholic* newspaper has revealed that fewer than 2% of Catholic schools (mostly in Dublin) were over-subscribed and therefore had to turn children away. Since the schools are Catholic schools established by the local parish, it is reasonable that where there are more applicants than places, priority is given to Catholic children. The debate is often framed as Catholic schools discriminating against non-Catholic children. However, the real crux of the debate is the Government's failure to provide an adequate number of school places in areas where the community is growing. In reality, the Government also needs to encourage more pluralism by funding more non-Catholic schools where there is a demand. It is sometimes claimed that the Church is opposed to this. However, it should be pointed out that it was the Archbishop of Dublin, Diarmuid Martin, who first proposed this. The Church, he pointed out, has no desire to be the default provider of education for Catholics and non-Catholics alike. At the same time, Catholic schools are at the forefront of welcoming children from all religious backgrounds and none. According to the Catholic Primary School Management Association (CPS-MA) in 2007, 95% of Catholic schools in the Republic accepted everyone who applied for admission. In fact, when Ireland became a destination for huge numbers of immigrants following the expansion of the European Union (EU) in 2004, Catholic schools were the first to reach out and provide language support and other services to help families integrate into the local community. It was Archbishop Diarmuid Martin, after all, who coined the term 'new Irish' to describe those – mostly from central and eastern Europe – who had decided to make Ireland their new home.

The Freedom to Love God

The Church's concern for individuals and business owners who want to be able to have and provide services and run businesses in ways that do not violate their consciences means preserving the freedom to bear witness to the Gospel.

In his homily during a March 2012 trip to Havana, Cuba, Pope Benedict listed the benefit to society of religious liberty. "Strengthening religious freedom consolidates social bonds, nourishes hope of a better world, and creates favourable conditions for peace and harmonious development, while at the same time establishing solid foundations for securing the rights of future generations."

It is worth fighting for.

■ EXISTING FRAME

> The Catholic Church seeks the right to discriminate against minorities by seeking exemptions from the law. Even though Catholics have a complete right to worship freely, they claim that their religious freedom is threatened. While they should be allowed to maintain their archaic, dogmatic and irrational views because everyone has freedom of belief and expression, they should not be given the freedom to impose them on others who do not share their views through their hospitals, schools and other social services. Nor should they be allowed to discriminate against gay people by refusing someone in a same-sex marriage the right to a job in a Catholic institution. The law is the law, and all are equal before it.

⟲ REFRAME

The Catholic Church is one of the world's leading advocates of equality and human rights, and believes nobody should be subject to unjust discrimination. This issue is not about the right to discriminate, but about the balance of freedoms in a modern pluralistic society — the need for some groups to be free from discrimination and the freedom to form organisations and witness to their beliefs. It is about how equality laws are framed in such a way that reflects that balance. The Church is not asking to be exempt from the law; it is asking for the law to be implemented differently for different groups, as happens already in many laws, in order to preserve a greater good. A healthy civil society hinges on the freedom of faith-based and other organisations with strong values to create and run those organisations in accordance with those values, as long as they don't inhibit other people's freedoms.

★ KEY MESSAGES

- Everyone has a home in the Church. Catholicism rejects unjust discrimination and prejudice against anyone because of his or her sexual orientation. The modern principle of equality has its roots in the Christian principle that all people are of equal value. The Catholic Church is globally one of the leading advocates of equality and rights — for the elderly, the unborn, immigrants, women and gay people. The Church does not oppose equality, but finds itself opposed to the way equality laws are sometimes implemented in the modern era in ways that negatively affect other rights and freedoms.

- Protecting minorities from unjust discrimination is one of the major tasks of the modern state. They remain fully subject to the law, but the law treats them differently.

- When the Church asks for exemptions, it is not trying to condition the law in accordance with its beliefs ('imposing its views') but appealing to a well-established principle in modern democracy and European rights law — the need to protect, in law, the freedom to associate and to manifest belief, which is the key·principle underlying the US Constitution. The corollary of a vigorous civil society is religious freedom.

Chapter 3

The 'Pelvic Issues': *Catholics and Human Sexuality*

Challenging Questions

- This is the twenty-first century; why does the Church still stick to the claim that sex must be about making children?
- Why does the Church call gay people 'disordered'? If God made them gay, why wouldn't he want them to have loving sexual relationships? Who are you to judge loving, consensual relationships?
- Shouldn't the Church be getting out of people's bedrooms and letting them make up their own minds about personal, sexual matters?

The Church's sexual teaching, vilified and mocked, stands in the road of contemporary culture like a great boulder: impossible to ignore and infuriatingly resistant to pressures to dislodge it. The ethics of autonomy — reinforced by consumerist messages — resist the idea of anyone telling us what to do with our lives, let alone our bodies. "Get out of our bedroom!" is the message the Church often receives. The idea that sex is not a morally neutral matter, that it expresses the deepest belonging between a man and a woman within a context of fidelity, permanence, and openness to life, is radically countercultural, for it insists, in keeping with the wisdom of ages and most cultures, that sex is for marriage. Those who live as if that were true are taking a brave stand. As New York's Cardinal Dolan put it in a January 2012 homily: "The one who, with God's grace and mercy, tries his or her best to be pure and chaste is often thought of not as a hero, not a saint, but as a freak in our culture today."

Yet just a generation or two ago it was not so. The jettisoning of the idea of sexual abstinence outside of marriage has occurred with astonishing speed in just a few decades, along with the widespread use of artificial contraception, the practice of abortion when that fails, the collapse of marriage, the spread of infidelity, the astonishing rise in divorce rates, and the implosion of the family. The 'sexual revolution' has also led to an outbreak of rape, pornography, child sexual abuse and profound loneliness and victimhood, hurting children and young women in a particularly shameful way.

As a result, there are signs of a turning tide; the current generation, having directly experienced the consequences of the meltdown of permanence in relationships, seeks something better. Most people in their hearts know that sex is or should be more than instant gratification between consenting adults, and long for trust and commitment. Pope Francis told young people during World Youth Day in Rio de Janeiro in July 2013:

> "In a culture of relativism and the ephemeral, many preach the importance of 'enjoying' the moment. They say that it is not worth making a lifelong commitment, making a definitive decision, 'forever', because we do not know what tomorrow will bring. I ask you, instead, to be revolutionaries, I ask you to swim against the tide; yes, I am asking you to rebel against this culture that sees everything as temporary and that ultimately believes you are incapable of responsibility, that believes you are incapable of true love. I have confidence in you and I pray for you. Have the courage 'to swim against the tide'. And also have the courage to be happy."

The challenge is to do so in a world where the model of a mother, father, and child living together in love can seem an impossible goal, and pointing to it can seem in itself judgmental. Jesus' teaching here is a genuine *skandalon*, a stumbling block to which the Church has added, in its teaching on marriage, its opposition to artificial means of contraception. The Church can very easily be framed as unrealistic — a great finger wagging 'no' to impulses of nature and the expression of love. When that finger belongs to a celibate priest, the frame is even harder to escape.

The issue is further inflamed because in the gay rights movement sexual freedom of expression has been blurred with the pursuit of civil rights for homosexual people, who traditionally have suffered real discrimination, so that anyone who questions the first is painted as an enemy of the second. That makes it particularly hard to communicate the message of the *Catechism of the Catholic Church*, which holds both that while gay and lesbian people "must be accepted with respect, compassion, and sensitivity" and all discrimination against them overcome, sexual relations between same-sex partners are acts of "grave depravity" and the homosexual inclination itself is "intrinsically disordered".

To many, this language is hurtful. It is heard as failing to take into account loving relationships between gay people and the sacrifices same-sex partners make to look after one another. Catholic teaching stands accused of contributing to a climate of intolerance. Teenagers and young adults with same-sex attractions who are still coming to terms with their sexual orientation are significantly more likely to attempt suicide or otherwise hurt themselves, and it is all too easy for critics to argue that lack of acceptance by the Church and intransigent Christian attitudes toward homosexuality contribute to this marginalisation.

Some time spent dwelling on the positive intention behind the critiques of the Church will help avoid unnecessarily reinforcing these frames. The positive intention draws on the sympathy for victims in a culture unconsciously imbued with the understanding of God as merciful. Our task is to show that, far from creating victims, a healthy understanding and use of sexuality is the only way to build lasting, fruitful relationships in which humanity — especially the vulnerable — finds its liberation.

✝ POSITIVE INTENTION ──────────────────────────────

Critics of the Church often start with pointing out the flaws and failures of a rigid sexual morality based on social convention and static social roles. A loveless marriage is not an argument against promiscuity, and the speed with which the family broke down in the West in the 1970s suggests that the society of the 1950s was no nirvana. There is also a puritanical strain in religious history which teaches that spirit is good and the flesh fallen; our culture is right to rebel against that idea, and to see the goodness in the physical — especially in sex.

Contraception is seen as protecting people from the consequences of their actions — unplanned pregnancy — that could affect the lives of many and create further victims.

The social marginalisation of gay people — who in the 1950s were offered chemical treatments to correct their 'problem' — is not something anyone wishes to return to.

We should have compassion for people who are not ready or willing to embrace conjugal love, especially in a culture where the models of permanence and fidelity are so few.

What Sex Is For

The sexual urge is not like hunger, where we need to eat or we die. The sexual urge comes from somewhere far deeper, from a longing for belonging and connection, and it has its vital place in building love between man and woman. As such, it is a precious, sacred gift, one with the capacity to bind and heal. Entered with reverence, in a spirit of unconditional self-surrender, it "awakens that which is most intimate, most sacred, most vulnerable in the human heart", as Jean Vanier, founder of L'Arche, writes in his *Man and Woman He Made Them*. Sex is mutual self-surrender that leaves a couple more deeply bound together than before, and brings forth a powerful gift to the world that makes it a far richer place.

At least it should be. But too often it is not. To unite physically where there is no unity of heart is hypocrisy; and when that happens, fairly soon the emotions will reflect a feeling of emptiness or anxiety. The contemporary, uncommitted sexual act — for pleasure, comfort, the relief of stress or a physical urge, or the expression of a hope that it will lead to commitment — is an occasion of great misery and pain. The feelings the morning after are a good guide. A sense of desolation suggests that sex has been separated from its purpose. Separated from the magnetism of love, sex turns us inward, and makes us endlessly self-obsessed — as the endless tortured relationship conversations among young people in any café will illustrate.

It is tempting to believe that the sexual act is a sign of commitment, but many a broken heart knows better. 'Hooking up' and casual sex too often lead to hurt, rejection and emptiness, deepening low self-esteem and cynicism. While the worst abuses of human sexuality override consent, even sexual activity that is 'consensual' can be, and often is, a source of suffering and emotional pain. Who has not known, or does not know another who has known, the searing sense of being treated as an object of desire, rather than an object of love?

Love entails a willingness to put another's needs before our own. It is self-surrender, a change in the way people focus their attention and energies, from the self to the other. When sex happens either without this change of heart or without this context of lifelong commitment, it can become simply an appetite with a tendency to treat persons as objects, which is why, perhaps, the modern experience of promiscuity is one of gratification followed quickly by boredom (people quickly tire of objects) and the feeling — by at least of one of the parties — of being 'used,' accompanied by a horrible sense that we have given away too much of ourselves. What we surrender in the sexual act is an intimate knowledge — the Bible describes sexual intercourse as 'knowing' — of ourselves that only those we trust and who love us should ever be allowed to access.

The misery, confusion, and anxiety surrounding uncommitted sex are, in themselves, proof that sex has an intrinsic meaning and purpose that have been forgotten. In ecology we speak of caring for nature, for respecting the created world, of not misusing what we have been entrusted with; human relationships, too, have an ecology. In the Church's understanding — one that has permeated our culture until recently — that purpose is linked to the very act of creation itself.

The Church holds that sexual activity is essentially 'good' if it has three elements:

a. it occurs within a lifelong, committed union;

b. it is between a man and a woman; and

c. it is open to children.

When sex fulfils these conditions, it conforms to God's design as being both 'procreative' and 'unitive'. These two meanings of the sexual act are mutually reinforcing. Sex that is open to life deepens the bond between man and woman precisely because it is open to life. That does not mean that every sexual act is, or can be, life-producing; beyond a certain age, it certainly won't be. But if the other conditions pertain, sex retains its intrinsic ecology.

This is an important point worth unpacking, since the Church's belief that "each and every marital act must of necessity retain its intrinsic relationship to the procreation of human life," as the 1968 encyclical *Humanae Vitae* puts it, is one of the hardest teachings of the Church today, one barely understood by many Catholics. But it is key.

In maintaining a firm connection between sexual activity and procreation, a couple is willing to open themselves to the possibility of being bound together for the rest of their lives by bringing a child into the world. Only that kind of commitment makes the relationship worthy for sex. This new life they will raise together, in partnership; the new person born as the fruit of their love will share their genes; and the couple, father and mother, man and wife, will be forever connected through their children and grandchildren. This is true 'lovemaking'.

It is precisely because of the power of sex that the Church seeks to protect it, and place boundaries around it, because that same power — the power to create life itself — can be highly destructive when it is loosed from its moorings. "Catholic doctrine and discipline may be walls," said G.K. Chesterton, "but they are the walls of a playground." He imagines a group of children playing on a high plateau; as long as there is a wall around them, they can play without fear. Without the wall, their fear of falling off the edge inhibits their ability to play. Loving, marital sex can be an occasion of joy and playfulness because it is boundaried; recreational, casual sex, lacking such boundaries, is chilled by anxiety, fear and emptiness.

The Catholic moral worldview tries to make sense not just of our biological, reproductive nature, but also of our nature as persons who find their ultimate fulfilment in the giving and receiving of love. While Church teaching on these matters is often seen as a 'no', it is actually quite the opposite. Marital love, *Humanae Vitae* explained, is

> "above all fully human, a compound of sense and spirit. It is not, then, merely a question of natural instinct or emotional drive. It is also, and above all, an act of the free will, whose trust is such that it is meant not only to survive the joys and sorrows of daily life, but also to grow, so that husband and wife become in a way one heart and one soul, and together attain their fulfilment."

This deep, compelling, uplifting teaching about the meaning and purpose of sex is very far from the banal idea of 'consent' taught by our law and culture. Consent tries to capture a good: sex should be an act of freedom, willingly entered into. But what is freedom in this context? Dawn Eden writes in *The Thrill of the Chaste*: "No matter how much I may love a man, if he and I refuse to vow ourselves to one another before Christ's representative, if we refuse to let the Holy Spirit seal our bond for as long as we both shall live, I am not truly free to make a gift of self to him."

True freedom in sexual matters, according to *Humanae Vitae*, is in knowing that a man and woman have vowed, in the sight of God, to "generously share everything, allowing no unreasonable expectations and not thinking solely of their own convenience".

Homosexuality

"Sexuality has an intrinsic meaning and direction, which is not homosexual," Pope Benedict XVI said in *Light of the World*, adding: "Evolution has brought forth sexuality for the purpose of reproducing the species." The purpose and meaning of sex is to unite a man and a woman in love in order to give children — and humanity — a future. "This is the determination internal to the essence of sexuality," Pope Benedict added. "Everything else is against sexuality's intrinsic meaning and direction."

That is what the Church means when it says that sex between two people of the same sex is "intrinsically disordered". Sex is inherently directed toward a particular purpose that cannot be fulfilled by sexual acts between same-sex partners. As the Congregation for the Doctrine of the Faith (CDF)'s 1986 *Letter to the Bishops of the Catholic Church on the Pastoral Care of Homosexual Persons* puts it: "It is only in the marital relationship that the use of the sexual faculty can be morally good."

It is not immoral or sinful, in other words, *to be gay*. As Cardinal Timothy Dolan puts it in John Allen's profile of him, *A People of Hope*: "Seen through the eyes of God, whatever your sexual attraction is, I don't really care too much about it. If you act on this attraction, it might diminish who you are, but I'm dealing with who you are and the way God sees you. If you see yourself as God sees you, well, you will act virtuously."

Because they are not 'complementary' — that is, between a man and a woman — same-sex sexual acts go against the grain of "the call to a life of that form of self-giving which the Gospel says is the essence of Christian living", says the Congregation for the Doctrine of the Faith (CDF), who immediately adds that this does not mean "that homosexual persons are not often generous and giving of themselves". It is homosexual acts, not gay people, that are incapable of that self-giving. The same can also be said of some sexual acts between a man and a woman, even in marriage. The difference is that sex between a man and a woman is ordered to self-giving, conjugal love — that is its purpose, its true nature — whereas a gay sexual act is incapable of being marital, and therefore is not ordered to the purpose of sexuality.

The language of disorder has often been misheard as describing gay *people* themselves. Yet "heterosexual persons not uncommonly have disordered sexual inclinations as well," say the US bishops in their 2006 document on pastoral care of gay people. "It is not enough for a sexual inclination to be heterosexual for it to be properly ordered." Pornography, adultery, or simply abusive sex are all examples of disordered heterosexual activity; as St Thomas Aquinas explained, "All sex between men and women outside legal marriage is intrinsically disordered."

So, while the word 'disordered' can sound highly offensive in light of the history of homophobic insults, it is a centuries-old technical term from moral theology that predates the existence of the modern science of psychiatry and has nothing to do with the medical persecutions of gay people of the nineteenth and early twentieth centuries. Homophobic language is directed at gay people themselves, and uses 'disordered' in the sense of 'unnatural'. Catholic teaching, on the other hand, is about the acts, not people. It is also the case that the word 'disordered' has no place in the Church's pastoral outreach to gay people or their families and friends. The use of the word in the *Catechism of the Catholic Church* is a reflection of the fact that this text is a master-catechism for bishops trained in philosophy and theology, and is intended to be transmitted into everyday language for everyday people. For example, the word 'disordered' does not appear in either the *Compendium* to the *Catechism* or the version aimed at young people, *Youcat*.

In fact, the Church takes no position on the unresolved 'nature versus nurture' debate about why some people are attracted to the same sex.

The *Catechism* simply notes that the genesis of homosexuality "remains largely unexplained". As then-Cardinal Ratzinger put it in an interview on the *Catechism* in 1997, "We have left room for all the hypotheses... whether [homosexuality] is innate or developed under certain circumstances." Generally, the Church prefers to speak of what sexuality is *for* rather than obsessing about what lies outside the boundaries of that vision. Pope St John Paul II, who wrote more about sexuality than all previous popes combined, alluded to homosexuality only briefly, and never in detail, during his *Theology of the Body*.

Why Contraception Is Wrong but NFP Isn't

Concerning contraception, the Catholic Church has maintained the traditional Christian teaching, expressed in *Casti Connubii* (Pius XI, 1931), that "since the conjugal act is destined primarily by nature for the begetting of children, those who in exercising it deliberately frustrate its natural power and purpose sin against nature." Pius XII upheld this teaching and developed it, allowing for the use of the infertile period to regulate births. At the Second Vatican Council, the role that sex plays in marriage in deepening 'conjugal love' between the husband and wife was stressed, along with the procreative element. This marked an important shift from a previous era in which marriage was seen primarily or sometimes exclusively as an institution for the fostering of children and for social stability. The 1968 encyclical *Humanae Vitae* developed the links between the two aspects, unitive and procreative, noting that "to experience the gift of married love while respecting the laws of conception is to acknowledge that one is not the master of the sources of life but rather the minister of the design established by the Creator".

Although any marriage deliberately closed to the possibility of children is invalid, the Church encourages married couples to discern how many children it is responsible and right for them to have. "Let them thoughtfully take into account both their own welfare and that of their children, those already born and those which the future may bring," the Catholic bishops of the world declared in the Second Vatican Council document *Gaudium et Spes*. Or, as Pope Francis put it in January 2015, while openness to life is a condition for the sacrament of matrimony, "the key word here is responsible parenthood and each person works out how to exercise this with the help of their pastor...Some people think that in order to be good Catholics we have to breed like rabbits! No: responsible parenthood".

The modern method recommended by the Church for spacing children is known as Natural Family Planning (NFP), of which there are a number of models or techniques. The spread and popularity of workshops and courses teaching these methods add up to a largely unreported 'quiet revolution' in contemporary society, similar, in some ways, to the rise in new habits of ecological awareness such as recycling; yet Catholics (less than 5% of whom use NFP) are almost as likely as everyone else to be ignorant of these techniques. They are at least as effective (and in most cases more effective) as contraceptive methods in enabling couples to plan births, yet unlike contraceptive methods, they do not suppress fertility. Natural Family Planning tracks a woman's fertility by measuring the presence and thickness of cervical mucus and body temperature, which are signs of ovulation. (There are various popular methods being taught, including the Creighton, Marquette, or Billings Ovulation models, and the 'Sympto-Thermal Method.' All claim 97–99% effectiveness). If the couple is trying to avoid a pregnancy, they then abstain from sex during times when ovulation is most likely. If they are trying to conceive, they will know the best times to try. It involves charts, measurements and lots of patience and communication.

Why is using this 'natural' method of preventing conception acceptable, but not 'artificial' methods? While there is much to be said about how much better (for people, for the planet) natural methods are, it is not because contraception is 'artificial' that the Church rejects it but because it severs the sexual act from its meaning. "The difference, both anthropological and moral, between contraception and recourse to the rhythm of the cycle, involves in the final analysis two irreconcilable concepts of the human person and of human sexuality," says the *Catechism*. The couple using NFP is accepting their fertility as it is: a great good, but a good that they are not going to use at this time; the husband respects his wife's cycle and does not try to manipulate it or suppress it. Whereas a couple using artificial birth control treats their fertility as an inconvenience, a defect in need of improvement, or an illness, a couple using NFP recognises fertility as a good and does nothing to deny this good. As Ashley McGuire writes: "It is in fact a great equaliser, because with NFP, the man can retain his fertility without making the woman shut hers off."

They also produce different kinds of behaviour. NFP requires self-restraint, the virtue of chastity developed through periodic abstinence that "brings to family life abundant fruits of tranquillity and peace," as *Humanae Vitae* observes. "It helps in solving difficulties of other kinds. It fosters in husband and wife thoughtfulness and loving consideration for one another. It helps them to repel inordinate self-love, which is the opposite of charity. It arouses in them a consciousness of their responsibilities. And finally, it confers upon parents a deeper and more effective influence in the education of their children."

Writing in *Commonweal* magazine in March 2015, Marian Crowe recalls how, after marrying in the 1960s, she quickly concluded that the Church was wrong about contraception and used it until after the birth of her third child before being sterilised. Looking back, she says,

"I now deeply regret both decisions. I believe that both the chemical contraception I used and the sterilisation harmed my body. There is evidence that at least some early forms of hormonal contraception increased the risk of diabetes, osteoporosis, and cervical, breast, and liver cancer. The IUD has been associated with menstrual problems and perforation of the uterus. Meanwhile, the more I have learned about Natural Family Planning — an updated and more effective version of the rhythm method — the more I have come to regret that I never tried it...Besides allowing one to avoid unnecessary chemicals, [NFP] cultivates self-discipline and fosters greater communication between spouses about their sexual life. It may even help us to appreciate and enjoy sex more, just as fasting can help us appreciate food. We regulate and humanise many aspects of our lives by imposing some discipline and order. To quote Chesterton, the proper form of thanks for the wondrous world in which we live is often 'some form of humility and restraint: we should thank God for beer and burgundy by not drinking too much of them. Maybe the best way to thank God for the gift of sexuality also involves restraint'."

The Call of Chastity

We are creatures of desire, not its prisoners. Saying 'no' to some desires and inclinations is the beginning of the moral life. That choice is what makes us capable of love. This is not a masochistic morality of stoic self-denial. We say 'no' to something as a step on the way to saying 'yes' to something even more important.

As Dawn Eden shows in *The Thrill of the Chaste*, chastity is "not a negative. Chastity is a virtue, and virtues are always positive. Virtues enable us to do things, aided by grace, that we would be unable to accomplish by our own power."

Exercising chastity is key to being able to live our sexuality because, paradoxical as it may seem, our sexual urge is not there just for sex. Properly understood and directed, it is the energy that helps us love — either chastely, or sexually. Chastity is "the virtue that enables us to love fully and completely in every relationship, in the manner that is appropriate to that relationship," writes Eden.

Our sexual urges, in other words, are not just for sex. As the *Catechism* puts it, sexuality "especially concerns affectivity, the capacity to love and to procreate, and in a more general way the aptitude for forming bonds of communion with others" (CCC 2332).

Relationships between people of the same gender by their nature need to be characterised by the love of friendship rather than erotic or romantic love. The Church does not ask gay people to refrain from love, but to love others of the same sex "fully and completely" in Eden's words, in the manner appropriate to relationships between two people of the same sex, precisely so that those relationships can be enjoyed more fully by those involved in them. The Church does not ask gay people to say 'no' to homosexual sex principally to protect a cultural institution that they cannot fully participate in (marriage). It does so in order for them to say 'yes' to the real good of same-sex love (friendship) most fully and completely.

The Church believes that sexuality has a deep interior meaning concerned with self-giving, one that is not restricted to the sexual act (which, given that most people most of the time are not having sex, should be good news). Note, in this passage from *The Truth and Meaning of Human Sexuality*, authored by the Pontifical Council for the Family (PCF), how the Church sees "friendship and self-giving", rather than marriage and sex, as the primary calling of the human person.

> "Love is [...] the fundamental and innate vocation of every human being...The person is thus capable of a higher kind of love than concupiscence, which only sees objects as a means to satisfy one's appetites; the person is capable rather of friendship and self-giving, with the capacity to recognise and love persons for themselves. Like the love of God, this is a love capable of generosity. One desires the good of the other because he or she is recognised as worthy of being loved...Man is called to love and to self-giving in the unity of body and spirit. Femininity and masculinity are complementary gifts, through which human sexuality is an integrating part of the concrete capacity for love which God has inscribed in man and woman...Insofar as it is a way of relating and being open to others, *sexuality has love as its intrinsic end, more precisely, love as donation and acceptance, love as giving and receiving.* The relationship between a man and a woman is essentially a relationship of love...When such love exists in marriage, self-giving expresses, through the body, the complementarity and totality of the gift. Married love thus becomes a power that enriches persons and makes them grow and, at the same time, it contributes to building up the civilisation of love."

Marriage is *one* way in which the meaning of the human body as a gift is expressed and lived out. But "each person" — not just those who are heterosexual or who are married — is "called to love as friendship and self-giving", and each and every person in turn "is freed from the tendency to selfishness by the love of others".

Marriage is a way of being in the world as an embodied, sexual person, but marriage is not the "intrinsic end" of human sexuality. Love is that end, a self-giving love which, according to the PCF, "generates communion between persons, because each considers the good of the other as his or her own good" — and to give generously of oneself is to live out the true inner meaning of one's sexuality, regardless of whether one is gay or straight, married or unmarried.

There are many ways in which this inner meaning of sexuality as a gift can be lived out that do not involve marriage: deep friendships; service of the poor, to the Church, and to society; dedication to family (caring for sick relatives); learning and teaching; involvement in the arts; serving the needy; getting involved in politics — all these are areas in which the unmarried, whether gay or not, have often produced great fruits. Precisely because marriage involves such an intense and absorbing commitment to only *one* other person and to children, those who are unmarried — gay or otherwise — may have particular opportunities for self-giving love that are closed to married people.

In the Church, religious orders and the priesthood are examples of such lives: the unmarried state creates space for self-giving that the vocation to marriage does not have room for. (St Paul made the case for celibacy in his first epistle to the Christians at Corinth when he told them, "The unmarried man is anxious about the affairs of the Lord, how to please the Lord; but the married man is anxious about worldly affairs, how to please his wife.") Many gay people have been, and are now, priests and religious, leading fulfilled lives of loving service to others.

A profound and lifelong friendship is not a consolation prize. The Christian tradition does not regard loving friendship (*philia*) as inferior to romantic love (*eros*) but a means to a greater end. The *Catechism* regards "disinterested friendship" as no less than the means to attain "Christian perfection". Or, as Eve Tushnet puts it in her book *Gay and Catholic*: "Jesus wasn't married. He didn't say, 'There is no greater love than this: to lay down one's life for one's wife.'"

Disinterested friendship is not cold but infused by the spirit of love that St Paul speaks about when writing to the Christians at Corinth — it "is not jealous or boastful," and it "does not insist on its own way" (I Corinthians 13:4–5). When lived out in this way, the *Catechism* says, "friendship represents a great good for all" that "leads to spiritual communion". (CCC 2347)

The Church's witness and mission, and the vibrancy of her inner life, would be truncated without the gifts that *both* married *and* unmarried people bring to the Church and the world. It does not follow that because a person does not marry they cannot live out the *deeper* meaning of their sexuality, which is to exist in the world as a loving gift to others. "In the evening of life, we will be judged on love alone," said St. John of the Cross.

In an increasingly individualistic and socially rootless society, marriage and romantic relationships have, perversely, come to be seen as the only means by which intimate and meaningful bonds of human connection can be formed and sustained. This affects not only gay people who choose to remain single, but — much more acutely — the elderly, those with physical and developmental disabilities, and other vulnerable groups. The fact that so many unmarried people are lonely and unhappy shows the need for our society to learn again the value of disinterested friendship, to push back against the individualistic "throwaway culture" deplored by Pope Francis.

Catholic teaching is demanding in this area. The *Catechism* itself acknowledges that gay people face a unique "trial" and a singular set of "difficulties". (CCC 2358). Yet sacrifice is the heart of love, and — as the resurrection of Jesus shows — can be transformed into a source of great joy and fruitfulness. "The love revealed by Christ," the PCF says in *The Truth and Meaning of Human Sexuality*, "is certainly a demanding love. But this is precisely the source of its beauty: by the very fact that it is demanding, it builds up the true good of man and allows it to radiate to others."

▪ EXISTING FRAME

The Church is obsessed with sexuality, whether heterosexual or gay. If God made people gay, isn't it terrible to condemn them to a life of celibacy? And why does the Church call gay people disordered? The Church's views on sex are outdated, and it's clear that many practising Catholics, particularly in the West, simply ignore its teaching.

↻ REFRAME

Sexual morality is about developing our capacity for self-giving love so that we don't use others. The proper context for sex is a lifelong commitment between husband and wife. The Church welcomes and embraces gay people. Many committed Catholics are gay, living faithful and chaste lives. Church teaching does not say gay people are disordered, but that sex is ordered to marriage and children. Both the Church and wider society would benefit from realising that there are many ways to live a happy and fulfilled life besides being married. Gay Catholics who follow Church teaching often offer fine examples of this forgotten truth.

★ KEY MESSAGES

- ▶ Sex should be open to children. That is the meaning of it. Sex is a blessing. It is a call to love. But it must be framed within commitment and stability — otherwise the body is lying.

- ▶ 'Limiting' sex to remaining open to procreation is not about restricting people's freedom, but about protecting and cherishing true love. Sex is a means of self-giving and this gift should be treated with respect.

- ▶ The Church does not call anyone disordered; it calls same-sex sex acts disordered, as are all sexual acts that are deliberately non-procreative.

- ▶ Sexuality is about self-giving, and there are many ways to give and receive love that are not sexual or marital. In a society that increasingly sees romantic unions as the only important interpersonal relationships in life, and yet in which many people are increasingly lonely and isolated, faithful gay Catholics provide a witness to the importance of nonsexual loving.

Chapter 4

The Church on the Frontier: Population, Development, AIDS, and Ecology

Challenging Questions

- Why doesn't the Church recognise that the effective use of condoms would save millions of lives in Africa from AIDS and allow millions more to escape from poverty?

- The planet cannot sustain current levels of population growth. Why can't the Church accept this scientific fact and promote birth control?

The Catholic Church, headed now by a Latin-American Pope, is mainly and increasingly a community of the global South. In the early 1900s, just 25% of the Catholic population lived outside Europe and North America. In the early twenty-first century, the reverse is true: 67% now live in Africa, Asia and Latin America. And by 2050, according to United Nations projections, seven of the ten largest Catholic countries will be on those continents. As wealthy countries' populations shrink, the population will continue to grow across the developing world. Some 95% of the increase will take place in developing countries, as is already happening: more than 90% of those less than 24 years of age live in the global South.

The Church is uniquely placed, as result, to articulate the views and the priorities of the poorest people of the world. And it is increasingly doing so on issues such as population control and the environment, while confronting vested interests and ideologies in the wealthy North. Referring to materialism and relativism at the 2009 Synod for Africa, for example, Pope Benedict XVI said it was "indisputable that the so-called 'first' world has sometimes exported and is exporting toxic spiritual refuse which contaminates the peoples of other continents, including in particular the population of Africa." Pope Francis, returning from Manila in January 2015, defended the freedom of developing countries to resist the "ideological colonisation" that seeks to impose birth control as the price for development assistance. His encyclical *Laudato Si'* is a bracing challenge to the wealthy countries to see that the destruction of the planet and the plight of the poor are part of the same problem, and that they must learn "to hear *both the cry of the earth and the cry of the poor*".

Yet issues such as population growth, birth control, poverty, development, and AIDS are often framed the opposite way — as a 'colonial' Church imposing practices and doctrines on the vulnerable poor that are inimical to their interests. The assumptions underlying this frame, driven by the ethics of autonomy of the North, are that overpopulation is the cause of poverty, and that women in the developing world need to be 'empowered' to have fewer children through birth control. This argument is bolstered by dire warnings about the planet being unable to sustain a burgeoning population. "Instead of resolving the problems of the poor and thinking of how the world can be different," writes Pope Francis in *Laudato Si'*, "some can only propose a reduction in the birth rate," adding

> "to blame population growth, instead of extreme and selective consumerism on the part of some, is one way of refusing to face the issues. It is an attempt to legitimise the present model of distribution, where a minority believes that it has the right to consume in a way that can never be universalised, since the planet could not even contain the waste products of such consumption."

This approach dominates the mindset of the United Nations agencies and has one of its most famous advocates in Melinda Gates, wife of multibillionaire Microsoft founder Bill Gates. Their foundation is putting vast sums into promoting contraception in developing countries, with a stated aim of giving 120 million women access to artificial birth-control methods (including sterilisation and abortion) by 2020. Gates, who is a Catholic at odds with her Church on this issue, believes that such methods are more 'modern' and effective than natural ones. Although she and other advocates of contraception put their case in terms of 'enabling women to choose' how many children to have, the messages of the educational programmes financed by the rich North carry a clear message: that fewer (poor) children are the passport to a better future. This 'neo-Malthusian' doctrine, as Pope Francis describes it, reflects a long-standing pessimism about the planet and population. Malthusianism is named after Thomas Malthus in the eighteenth century, who argued that without war, pestilence, and famine, human numbers would always outstrip food production. His deep pessimism about the capacity of the earth to sustain population growth has been disproved by history; economists have shown that in spite, and even because of, population growth the state of the world has improved, and there is no reason to think that it will not continue to do so.

The clash between the Church's worldview and that of the agencies of the wealthy North has been particularly evident in the question of the HIV/AIDS pandemic, the greatest threat to Africa since the slave trade. According to UNAIDS (2016), about 25.5 million sub-Saharan Africans have the virus — almost 70% of the total global HIV-infected population of 36.7 million. Between 2000 and 2020, about 55 million Africans will have died of AIDS-related diseases. The pandemic has decimated the population, wiping out half of the working-age people in many areas, leaving grandparents to care for their orphaned grandchildren.

Most people in Western countries think that, just as the widespread use of condoms contributed to bringing down rates of HIV transmission among gay men in the US and Western Europe in the 1980s, the 'answer' to AIDS in Africa must be more of the same. Yet HIV (the virus that causes AIDS) in Africa has different characteristics, and a deluge of evidence points to the ineffectiveness of campaigns encouraging people to have 'safe sex'.

The Church's alternative policy — encouraging responsible sexual behaviour while tackling the stigma of AIDS and poverty — is born not just of moral conviction but also of knowledge of the realities of Africa on the ground. To the secular Western mind, however, it seems just the opposite: the imposition by detached dogmatists of a religious doctrine. As a result, Catholics find themselves admonished for 'contributing to the spread of the virus', 'sacrificing innocent lives on the altar of dogma', and even 'being directly responsible for the deaths of millions of Africans'.

Yet it is now even more clear that it is the 'more condoms' approach that betrayed a detached, even colonialist, mentality. Abstinence programmes, on the other hand, by appealing to traditional cultural and religious values deeply embedded in the peoples of the developing world, have a proven track record of success in curbing the spread of the virus. The early strategy of the UNAIDS programme was based on a fatal misreading of African realities. In his 2003 book *Rethinking AIDS Prevention*, the anthropologist and Harvard expert Edward C. Green attributes this disaster to the mindset of the mainly European and American health experts who advise governments on their policies for combating AIDS.

Many of today's international health bureaucracies were established in the 1970s, when the governments of rich countries, fearing the population explosion in poor countries, poured money into programmes to promote contraception. The Church argued against those flawed strategies from the start, and Blessed Pope Paul VI's *Humanae Vitae* was a prophetic attempt to resist the neo-Malthusian ideology underlying them.

The criticism of the Church concerning this issue begins with a positive intention which all should share: the scandal of gross poverty, the need to save lives, and the idea that the best solutions are those that are within the desires of the culture concerned. But the grand irony is that while the Church is accused of resisting Western artificial contraception because it is imposing its dogma, the exact reverse is true. The Church speaks on these questions with a unique authority born of close knowledge of the realities on the ground: no other organisation has such a presence in the most remote villages and in the poorest slums; none has had such intense involvement on the frontline of prevention and treatment in sub-Saharan Africa and other developing countries; no single civil-society organisation can match the Church's level of activity among the poor. Conversely, the birth-control programmes financed and administered by the international bureaucracies begin with ideologies and assumptions distant from the lived realities and culture of the poor. Not only are those programmes imposed, but the massive resources being deployed by rich countries to urge poor countries to have fewer children are a distraction from the real needs of those countries.

"I see this $4.6 billion buying us misery," writes Obianuju Ekeocha, a Nigerian Catholic activist, in a letter to Melinda Gates in response to news of her 'donation'. "I see it buying us unfaithful husbands. I see it buying us streets devoid of the innocent chatter of children. I see it buying us disease and untimely death. I see it buying us a retirement without the tender loving care of our children. Please Melinda, listen to the heartfelt cry of an African woman and mercifully channel your funds to pay for what we *really* need."

POSITIVE INTENTION

Millions of people in Africa are in danger of being infected and sooner or later dying of AIDS. Saving lives must come first. The population explosion in the developing world is putting a great strain on resources. People need a route out of poverty. The best solutions are those that come out of the cultural horizon of those involved.

The Church and AIDS

Helen Epstein, a Jewish-American journalist and author of a highly praised 2007 book on the AIDS virus, *The Invisible Cure*, notes that "Catholic and Protestant churches had been running exemplary AIDS programmes in Africa since the 1980s". No organisation has been closer to and more involved with the communities afflicted by AIDS than the Catholic Church. And no organisation has been more effective in tackling AIDS at its root.

Along with Protestant churches, the Catholics were on the frontlines as soon as the epidemic began, responding to the imperative to care for the suffering and dying and to educate the human family in ways to prevent the further spread of HIV. Today, often in partnership with others, they play a vital and expanding role in the comprehensive response to HIV across the developing world: assisting people in avoiding infection; providing tests to find out if people are infected and offering physical and spiritual care to those who are; working in communities to combat stigmatisation and discrimination; caring for those affected (especially widows and orphans); helping those infected to live positively; and advocating on behalf of persons living with HIV or AIDS. This largescale service of a suffering population has given rise to theological reflection. So closely do Catholics identify with those infected that some speak of the Church itself 'living with AIDS'.

Catholic AIDS programmes work through existing diocesan and parish structures; they do not come from 'outside'. The Church is not an NGO providing a service for foreigners; the Church is the people. Bishop Kevin Dowling of Rustenberg, former chair of the Southern African Catholic Bishops' Conference (SACBC) AIDS office, notes how the Church's response "is intimately linked to its mission in the world, a response which must be based on and reveal fundamental Gospel attitudes, values, such as compassion, solidarity, care for the vulnerable, striving for justice, and commitment to overcoming unjust structures in society."

Leaving aside its many other qualifications to speak on this issue, therefore, the number and reach of its programmes mean the Church deserves to be recognised as the world's leading voice on AIDS: around the world the Church ministers to more than 25% of all those with the virus, a figure that rises to 50 or 75% in Africa, and in many remote areas, close to 100%. As the Church has long pointed out, while condom use can be effective in reducing HIV transmission within identifiable high-risk sub-groups (prostitutes, gay men), it has the opposite effect in the population at large, where the greater availability and use of condoms cause infection rates to escalate.

AIDS and Condoms

Let us begin with those cases — prostitutes and so on — where condom use can be effective in reducing the risk of AIDS. Does the Church tell, say, a woman who is selling her body to feed her children not to insist on the use of condoms? What of those who are not ready or are unable to embrace monogamy, fidelity, and abstinence; should the Church urge them to use condoms as prophylactics, where the intention is to prevent death rather than life? These cases do not involve the Church's teaching on contraception, which is a teaching about the use of sexuality within marriage (see Chapter 3). Pope Benedict intervened in this discussion in November 2010 when he cited the case of a prostitute who chooses to use a condom in order to avoid infecting someone, interpreting this act of care as the possible beginning of a journey of moral awakening. The Congregation for the Doctrine of the Faith later added that "those involved in prostitution who are HIV positive and who seek to diminish the risk of contagion by the use of a condom may be taking the first step in respecting the life of another — even if the evil of prostitution remains in all its gravity."

This is not a Pharasaical position; the Church knows that such situations are morally complex, and anybody facing difficult moral choices will receive pastoral support from the Church. But the objective of such support will be to guide people toward what is right — and what is most effective in combatting the disease — fidelity, monogamy and abstinence.

In general, however, condoms cannot solve AIDS in Africa. AIDS is "a tragedy that cannot be overcome by money alone, and that cannot be overcome by the distribution of condoms, which even aggravates the problems," as Pope Benedict XVI put it to journalists on his way to Cameroon in March 2009. The remarks caused a hailstorm of outrage. Yet Cameroon itself dramatically illustrated the truth of his remarks: between 1992 and 2001, condom sales in Cameroon increased from six million to 15 million while HIV infection rates tripled, from 3% to 9%.

Dr Edward C. Green of Harvard University — the author of five books and 250 peer-reviewed articles, widely considered the world's greatest expert on the issue — said the Pope was "actually correct". James Shelton of the US Agency for International Development said so too, writing in the *Lancet* that "condoms alone have limited impact in generalised epidemics". No country in Africa has yet turned back a generalised epidemic by means of condom distribution.

In a May 9, 2008, article for *Science* magazine, ten AIDS experts criticised the way most of the United States' $3.2 billion UNAIDS budget was allocated to condoms-based interventions, arguing that "partner reduction" was the key to curbing AIDS, as the Church had long argued.

The reason is clear from Epstein's study, *The Invisible Cure*, which showed how 'concurrency' — having multiple, long-term sexual partners — was the key reason why HIV rates exploded in Africa despite increased condom use. Although the evidence for this was everywhere, the reluctance to translate it into international policies was, as her book devastatingly shows, due to resistance on the part of Western liberals to introduce programmes of moral behaviour that would challenge their own values.

In Africa the main reason why the AIDS epidemic exploded was the prevalence of multiple committed, long-term relationships that act as a 'superhighway' for the virus. As Epstein puts it: "AIDS is common in Africa not because African people have so many sexual partners, but because they are more likely than people in other world regions to have a small number of concurrent long-term partners. This places them, along with their partner or partners, within a vast network of ongoing sexual relationships that is highly conducive to the spread of HIV."

This is why contraception campaigns, such as the one promoted by Melinda Gates, only exacerbate that problem. While condoms can be effective in reducing the spread of the virus in casual sexual encounters, they are seldom used in long-term, stable relationships, which is where most of the AIDS transmission in Africa occurs.

Reducing the number of partners — or, as the Church urges, fidelity and monogamy in marriage — has, conversely, been dramatically effective. In Zimbabwe and Kenya, for example, the HIV rate began to decline in the late 1990s as the number of multiple partnerships fell; but in Botswana, South Africa, and Lesotho, where no partner reduction occurred in the 1990s and where condoms were emphasised as the main method of prevention, HIV rates soared.

Dr Green — an agnostic scientist — was one of a handful of experts who for years had been arguing that faithfulness was the key to combating the virus. Side-lined and ignored in the 1990s, they now represent mainstream scientific opinion, although the Western media — reflecting the ignorance of the wider society — has been slow to catch on.

As Fr Michael Czerny, former director of the African Jesuit AIDS Network (AJAN) puts it, "The promotion of condoms as the strategy for reducing HIV infection in a general population is based on statistical probability and intuitive plausibility. It enjoys considerable credibility in the Western media and among Western opinion makers. What it lacks is scientific support."

Condoms-based campaigns carry an implicit pessimism about human beings, seeing people as rapacious, unable to control themselves, and incapable of moving beyond self-gratification. It is also an attitude alien to traditional African values. Imposed by international agencies on Africans, it represents, says Fr Czerny, an "unconscious racism".

The Catholic Church in southern Africa runs programmes that appeal to traditional African social values. The Church's conviction is that the virus must be tackled through the 'humanisation of sexuality', based on faith in God and respect for oneself and others, in contrast to the 'banalisation of sexuality' implicit in condom campaigns. Its prevention programmes are highly effective in educating young people to resist sexual advances and to abstain until marriage. A large part of the effectiveness of the Church's anti-HIV programmes lies in their community-based approach, depending on a large network of volunteers with strong values and a dedication to helping others.

Sound epidemiological research supports the Church's approach. As Dr Green writes: "As evidence mounts about the high prevalence and deadly nature of multiple and concurrent partnerships, we must reorient prevention interventions and research to promote behaviour change — in particular, partner reduction and sexual exclusivity." The classic example is Uganda, where HIV prevalence declined from 21% to 9.8% in the 1990s following a reduction in non-regular sexual partners by 65%. That shift in behaviour was the result of a government-backed, community-based campaign supported by the churches. Behavioural change — according to a 2004 report in the journal *Science* by authors Stoneburner and Low-Beer — was the crucial factor. "The major difference in Uganda is a reduction in non-regular sexual partners and an associated contraction of sexual networks."

This approach is the most effective, the most realistic and the most successful. And there is no alternative. As the Catholic bishops of Africa put it in their message at the end of the Second Synod for Africa (October 2009): "The problem cannot be overcome by the distribution of prophylactics. We appeal to all who are genuinely interested in arresting the sexual transmission of HIV to recognise the success of programmes that propose abstinence among those not yet married, and fidelity among the married. Such a course not only offers the best protection against the spread of this disease but is also in harmony with Christian morality."

Why People Aren't the Problem

The example of AIDS illustrates the dangers of the 'ideological colonisation' Pope Francis warns about. Well-meaning attempts to reduce poverty and disease can cause great harm when driven by narrow-minded, wealthy-culture assumptions shaped by the ethic of autonomy. The same dogmatism underlies the fixed ideas of international agencies that the cause of poverty is overpopulation, and that all they have to do to escape poverty is have fewer children.

"If you don't have oil," Norway's Minister of Development Heikki Holmas told developing country representatives, "your future lies in family planning." He was speaking at a 2012 conference in London opened by the world's richest woman, Melinda Gates, who said the goal of her campaign was to "increase demand for contraception" because "what we know from the demographic dividend is that around the world, the transition from a low-income to middle-income country happens when parents have fewer children."

There is a host of assumptions here: some erroneous and simplistic, others sinister. One of them is that population growth retards economic growth. While it is true that some very poor countries have high populations, and demography can be a challenge for development, the link is not causal: from the nineteenth century onward, there was a rapid growth in per capita incomes that matched the spectacular growth in population, and it remains the case that the countries with the highest rates of economic growth and savings are those with the largest populations. Rapid population growth has not been an obstacle to rapid economic development, whether in the United States in the past or in India now, and is usually considered economically beneficial. The converse is also true: in wealthy countries, the long-term prospects where the birth-rate remains well below replacement level (2.1 children per woman) are grim: the demographic collapse that began in the 1970s has led to low birth-rates, ageing populations, and shrinking numbers of workers, causing an economic time-bomb for many countries.

What normally happens is that as per capita incomes grow fertility falls. The best contraceptive, it is sometimes said, is education for girls — something the Church provides across the developing world. The key resource is human beings; we are the solution rather than the problem. In the modern view, the growth in per capita income during the past 150 years has little to do with population, but rather is caused by the accumulation of human and physical capital and the discovery of new technologies. According to a 2010 article in the *American Economic Review* by leading researchers, "larger populations encourage greater specialisation and increased investments in knowledge, mediated in part through bigger and more important cities."

The spectre of unsustainable population growth is based on old data. Now, the experts are speaking of a second demographic transition known as the 'New Demography'. Sometime in the twenty-first century the world will begin depopulating, a phenomenon that has already hit Western Europe and Japan. One scenario posited by the UN, which assumes that fertility rates will stabilise at 1.85 — considerably beneath the replacement level of 2.1 — puts the global population in 2300 at 2.3 billion, a rather different prospect than the nine billion the population controllers claim.

Whatever the future of the world's population, it doesn't take away from the scandal of real poverty in many parts of the world now. In poor, agricultural economies with limited capital, poor infrastructure, and rudimentary technology, higher populations do go hand in hand with low per capita incomes. In developing countries, says Pope Francis in *Laudato Si'*, "access to ownership of goods and resources for meeting vital needs is inhibited by a system of commercial relations and ownership which is structurally perverse." What to do about this? The *Catechism* says: "Rich nations have a grave moral responsibility toward those which are unable to ensure the means of their development by themselves or have been prevented from doing so by tragic historical events." (CCC 2439)

Put simply, the Church believes that rich nations should increase the availability of resources to the poor while family planners believe that rich nations should reduce the number of human beings using resources.

The idea that women of colour in the global South are victims of their own fertility — that they are the reason for their poverty — carries the unmistakable whiff of racism and colonialism. In *Sollicitudo Reo Socialis*, Pope St John Paul II deplored the way governments and agencies in the rich nations were carrying out "systematic campaigns against birth contrary not only to the cultural and religious identity of the countries themselves but also contrary to the nature of true development." Deploring "the absolute lack of respect for the freedom of choice of the parties involved, men and women often subjected to intolerable pressures, including economic ones, in order to force them to submit to this new form of oppression," he noted how it was the poorest populations of the world that suffer such mistreatment. He saw behind such birth-control campaigns "a form of racism, or the promotion of certain equally racist forms of eugenics".

Pope Francis refers to this as 'ideological colonisation' with good reason: it is a mindset that is authoritarian and coercive. The problem, as with the approach to AIDS, is a narrow view that sees life as inimical to development, and which results in resources being channelled away from where they are truly needed. People working in the field have long deplored the way basic diseases, which cost pennies to treat, are ignored, while millions of dollars of contraceptives are available.

Again in *An Open Letter to Melinda Gates*, Obianuju Ekeocha described how the real needs of her remote rural community could be transformed by investment in what the people genuinely needed, which above all is good prenatal, neonatal, and paediatric care. Women are not dying because they are having too many children but because they are not getting basic post-partum care; what was needed was birthing centres with neonatal units. And if women wanted to space their children, they should have Natural Family Planning methods taught, which cost little and caused no health side-effects. She went on to call for Gates to fund nurseries for young children where they could be fed and taught while their parents worked; chastity programmes for young women to counter promiscuous messages from Western media and to resist the spread of HIV; microbusinesses that help women accumulate know-how and capital; and help for existing cash-starved NGOs that protect women from sex-trafficking, prostitution, forced marriage, child labour, domestic violence and sex crimes.

"$4.6 billion dollars can indeed be your legacy to Africa and other poor parts of the world," she told Gates. "But let it be a legacy that brings life, love, and laughter into the world in need."

"Openness to life is at the centre of true development," writes Benedict XVI in *Caritas in Veritate*. It is the mindset that allows for government policies and the efforts of individuals and organisations to attend to the true needs of the poor rather than trying to defend the interests of the rich. "By cultivating openness to life, wealthy peoples can better understand the needs of poor ones, they can avoid employing huge economic and intellectual resources to satisfy the selfish desires of their own citizens, and instead, they can promote virtuous action within the perspective of production that is morally sound and marked by solidarity, respecting the fundamental right to life of every people and every individual."

Integral Ecology

The Church, which knows the lives of the world's poor better than any international agency or organisation, urges what Pope Francis called (in an address in September 2013) "an authentic and integral development" that aims "to provide dignified living conditions for everyone, at finding just responses to the needs of individuals and families, and at ensuring that God's gift of creation is respected, safeguarded, and cultivated".

Bringing about that better world is not just a question of rich countries spending more on aid and development. It requires a conversion on the part of those nations that dominate the world economy. "An economic system centred on the god of money needs to plunder nature to sustain the frenetic rhythm of consumption that is inherent to it," Pope Francis told a meeting of landless farmers and informal workers in October 2014, adding: "The monopolising of lands, deforestation, the appropriation of water, inadequate agro-toxics are some of the evils that tear man from the land of his birth. Climate change, the loss of biodiversity, and deforestation are already showing their devastating effects in the great cataclysms we witness."

Drawing on the teachings of previous popes, Pope Francis has, in *Laudato Si'*, made it no longer optional to be a Catholic and not care for the environment. The damage to the planet — the depletion of the ozone layer and rising world temperatures as a result of greenhouse gases — is symptomatic of lifestyles that need to be challenged as materialistic and self-focused. Humanity "is called to recognise the need for changes of lifestyle, production, and consumption, in order to combat this warming or at least the human causes which produce or aggravate it."

The environmental devastation affects the poor above all, who die young in conflicts over resources, yet this is barely noticed because "many professionals, opinion makers, communications media, and centres of power, being located in affluent urban areas, are far removed from the poor". A true ecological approach, says Pope Francis, "always becomes a social approach; it must integrate questions of justice in debates about the environment, so as to hear both the cry of the earth and the cry of the poor."

Between 1.2 and 1.5 billion people are still mired in 'extreme poverty'. Global inequalities continue to widen. Sub-Saharan Africa has the second highest rate of economic growth in the world (after developing Asia) yet remains locked in a negative cycle of poverty and underdevelopment. The wealth of the top one percent has grown 60% in the last twenty years.

Millions of hectares of forest are lost every year, many species are being driven closer to extinction, and renewable water resources are becoming scarcer. By 2030, only 10% of the forests that once covered the earth will remain, leading to loss of species and increasing carbon dioxide. Protecting the Amazon has become a national crusade for the Brazilian Church.

It is not large families that cause poverty, and poverty cannot be 'solved' by persuading the poor to have fewer children. Nor can we rely on technology to solve the challenge of global warming and environmental degradation. What has to change is an economic culture that puts money and profit ahead of people, and a "technocratic mentality," as *Laudato Si'* puts it, that "perceives reality as something that can be manipulated endlessly".

Modernity has been marked by an "excessive anthropocentrism". A correct relationship with the world requires restoring our place in relation to others as well as to God. Linking the culture of relativism to the "throwaway culture", Francis sees the "same disorder" behind forced labour, the sexual exploitation of children, and the abandonment of the elderly, as well as "the disordered desire to consume more than what is really necessary". Combatting these ills means caring for the whole of life and the whole of creation. Concern for the protection of nature is also incompatible with the justification of abortion, he notes, for "how can we genuinely teach the importance of concern for other vulnerable beings... if we fail to protect a human embryo?"

Francis calls instead for "an approach to ecology that respects our unique place as human beings in this world and our relationship to our surroundings." Integral ecology sees the environmental and social crises not as separate but as two facets of the same crisis. Thus, 'cultural ecology' involves respect for place and the past and the rights of peoples and their cultures, while an "ecology of daily life" involves creating better conditions for "belonging and togetherness" as well as improving transport and housing. "Human ecology," meanwhile, acknowledges the link between human life and the moral law, inscribed in our nature, beginning with our bodies. Francis contrasts the acceptance of our bodies as God's gift with "thinking we enjoy absolute power over our bodies", which soon becomes "thinking that we enjoy absolute power over creation". In a critique of gender theory, Francis observes that "valuing one's own body in its femininity or masculinity is necessary if I am going to be able to recognise myself in an encounter with someone who is different."

Francis sees the origin of the problem in a sinful mindset that puts human beings, rather than God, in authority over the earth, thereby confusing dominion with exploitation rather than stewardship, in which the world was entrusted to man for him to cultivate and care for. The only way to restore men and women to their rightful place, he says, "is to speak once more of the figure of a Father who creates and who alone owns the world." Only when we acknowledge the value and fragility of nature will we "finally leave behind the modern myth of unlimited material progress" and create what he calls "a sound ethics, a culture and spirituality genuinely capable of setting limits and teaching clear-minded self-restraint".

Laudato Si' spells out an ecological conversion involving "new convictions, attitudes, and forms of life" that will set us out on the "long path of renewal". Noting that when people become self-centred and self-enclosed "their greed increases", the Pope calls for society to "acknowledge our deep dissatisfaction and embark on new paths to authentic freedom". The Pope asks that environmental education be open to the transcendent, requiring educators to help people grow in solidarity, responsibility, and compassionate care. The conversion starts with changes in lifestyle and consumer choices in daily life: recycling waste, turning off lights, and wearing warmer clothes to use less heating. Such efforts "benefit society, often unbeknown to us, for they call forth a goodness which, albeit unseen, inevitably tends to spread." These habits and gestures begin, above all, in the family, where we learn "respect for the ecosystem and care for all creatures". "Our efforts at education will be inadequate and ineffectual," warns the Pope, "unless we strive to promote a new way of thinking about human beings, life, society, and our relationship with nature. Otherwise the paradigm of consumerism will continue to advance, with the help of the media and the highly effective workings of the market."

◼ EXISTING FRAME

The Church's attempts to impose its sexual dogmas on poor countries have led to overpopulation and contributed to the spread of AIDS.

↻ REFRAME

No organisation is as present among the world's poor as the Catholic Church, defending the interests of the poor against attempts by wealthy countries to persuade them to have fewer children. Church AIDS programmes do not just promote that which is morally right and works best, but which fits with the values of traditional societies. From the standpoint of its option for the poor, the Church critiques a world economy too geared to the satisfaction of the materialist desires of the rich rather than the needs of the poor, and promotes an "integral ecology" capable of responding to the interconnected issues of "human ecology", development, and the environment.

★ KEY MESSAGES

▶ The Church is uniquely placed to articulate the views and the interests of the poorest people of the world and speaks on their behalf with genuine authority.

▶ The Church's AIDS prevention policy — encouraging responsible sexual behaviour, above all in reducing partners — is born not just of moral conviction but of knowledge of the realities of AIDS in Africa on the ground. It has been vindicated by the world's leading experts on the issue.

▶ The massive resources being deployed by rich countries to urge poor countries to have fewer children are a distraction from the real needs of those countries.

▶ Well-meaning attempts to reduce poverty and disease can cause great harm when driven by narrow-minded, wealthy cultures' assumptions shaped by the ethics of autonomy. The same dogmatism underlies the fixed ideas of international agencies that the cause of poverty is overpopulation. The Church believes that rich nations should increase the availability of resources to the poor, not reduce the number of human beings using resources.

▶ Openness to life is at the centre of true development. It is not large families that cause poverty, and poverty cannot be 'solved' by persuading the poor to have fewer children. What has to change is an economic culture that puts money and profit ahead of people and that puts satisfying consumer demands in wealthy countries before the basic needs of those in poor countries. The consequences are evident in climate change.

▶ To tackle these interrelated challenges, we need an 'integral ecology'.

Chapter 5

Protecting the Foundations: *Promoting Marriage*

Challenging Questions

- Gay people these days often live in stable, loving relationships, and can raise their own children adopted or created through surrogacy. Why shouldn't they also be allowed to marry?

- Homosexual parenting already exists as a matter of fact: Hundreds of thousands of children are being raised by gay couples. Surely a legal framework must exist to protect these children?

- Marriage is about love. Are you saying gay people can't love each other, or their children, as much as straight people?

- There was opposition in the 1950s to interracial marriage. The Church opposes marriage between same-sex couples now. If it was bigotry then, why isn't it bigotry now?

- Religious people can marry in churches, but what right does the Church have to impose its understanding of marriage on non-believers?

The dismantling of marriage as a conjugal institution by the state is one of the most rapid and far-reaching social and political developments of our time. The first country to permit two individuals of the same sex to marry each other was the Netherlands in 2001. Belgium followed two years later. In 2005, they were joined by Canada — which redefined marriage as "the lawful union of two persons to the exclusion of all others". Next came Spain, and before 2010 was over, South Africa, Portugal, Argentina, Norway, Sweden and Iceland had all followed suit. As of March 2018, twenty-five countries had passed 'marriage equality' laws. In 2015, Ireland became the first country in the world to legalise same-sex marriage by way of a referendum which amended the Constitution to state that "marriage may be contracted in accordance with law by two persons without distinction as to their sex". In the US, following a Supreme Court ruling in 2015, marriage is now a constitutional right in all 50 states.

The lightning advance of same-sex marriage is the result not just of energetic and well-funded lobbying by interest groups, but of the evangelical ardour with which it has been promoted by politicians, celebrities and business leaders under the banner of equality and fairness, the rallying cry of the ethics of autonomy. For its advocates, same-sex marriage is the latest iteration in the civil rights movement and the historic emancipation of gay people, a history that began with the lifting of laws criminalising homosexual acts and the introduction of laws banning discrimination against gay people in the workplace. This frame is so powerful that anyone questioning same-sex marriage automatically finds themselves on the defensive — having to explain that they are not bigots opposed to equality, or loving relationships, or civil rights for gay people.

The frame appears to be coherent because same-sex marriage follows from a long series of legal gains for gay rights since the Stonewall riots of 1969 in New York. The gay-rights movement has moved from securing the right to protection from criminalisation and marginalisation — freedom from discrimination, which the Church supported and continues to support — to securing legal rights and privileges such as inheritance rights, hospital visitation rights, tax breaks, and so on, often through civil-partnership arrangements. In many countries – including Ireland – the movement has succeeded in securing the legalisation of same-sex adoption too, which involves overriding the right of children to a mother and a father.

Same-sex marriage can appear to flow logically from these previous gains, and this is how it has successfully been framed. Thus, the restriction of marriage to a man and a woman is seen as a form of archaic discrimination, and same-sex marriage is seen as flowing from society's commitment to equality; to oppose it is therefore to suppress a right. As a result, opposition to it is now characterised, at best, as clinging to 'old-fashioned' religious beliefs and traditions, and at worst as homophobia and hatred. The Church, which has been vigorous in its opposition to same-sex marriage, is further accused of seeking to impose its 'religious' view of marriage on 'secular' laws.

Yet only about 25 of the 193-member states of the United Nations had adopted same-sex marriage by 2018, and for the overwhelming majority of the world marriage remains a male-female union centred on children. That was also the view, until just a few years ago, of the gay-rights movement itself. The idea of a 'right' of a same-sex couple to marry seldom occurred to anyone in the civil rights marches of the 1950s–60s, and no such 'right' exists in any charter of international law, something the European Court of Human Rights (ECHR) has repeatedly pointed out. The state acts lawfully in seeking to defend, in law, the traditional understanding of marriage as between a man and a woman.

Some have tried to portray these constitutional obstacles as analogous to the attempts to ban miscegenation — marriage between different races — in some southern US states in the 1950s. But it has always been a human right — one enshrined in every charter of rights — for any adult man to marry any adult woman if they are free to do so, across the boundaries of race and faith and culture. The anti-miscegenation laws were the suppression of a human right that only racists could approve of, and which were offensive to the civil rights movement.

Ironically, same-sex marriage is very much like those anti-miscegenation laws in seeking to redefine the very institution of marriage. That is why invoking the language of civil rights is simply not appropriate; this is not about granting a minority access to the benefits of a social institution, because in order to do so the very nature of the institution must be essentially changed. Same-sex marriage requires the state to declare that marriage is no longer a conjugal institution, one founded on the fertile union of a man and a woman and for the raising of their natural children, but rather a mere contract between consenting individuals in which the elements that define marriage — procreation, fertility, fidelity, and permanence — are irrelevant or incidental. The slogan 'equal marriage' suggests equality of access to the same institution; in reality, it means making marriage equal to non-marital relationships.

The fact that this is barely noticed in the discussion indicates just how far the cultural meaning of marriage has broken down in wealthy Western nations. In the US, throughout the 1940s, 50s, and early 60s, men and women paired off, raised children as a unit, and more or less stuck together for life. In 1965, when the Moynihan Report was issued, there was deep alarm at the out-of-wedlock birth rate for African-Americans of 25%; to-day 40% of all children, 50% of Hispanics and 70% of African-Americans are born outside of marriage. In Ireland today, more than 34% of births are outside marriage – in socially disadvantaged communities this rises to over 50%, which makes the link between children and marriage seem tenuous, while widespread divorce and infidelity make it harder to see the connection between permanence and faithfulness. In Ireland, the num-ber of people with broken marriages has risen from 40,000 in 1986 to 280,000 in 2016. As Pope Francis told journalists in May 2014: "Young people no longer want to get married, or prefer simply to live together; marriage is in crisis, and therefore the family is too."

It is this collapse of culture's grasp of the meaning of marriage, not the advance of civil rights, that explains same-sex marriage. Little sur-prise, in this context, that a new 'partnership' model of marriage should be advanced, in which gender complementarity and procreation — the most basic of all elements of marriage — should be dismissed as inciden-tal. Only in cultures transfixed by the ethic of autonomy has government after government enacted legislation that permanently enshrines in law an eviscerated version of marriage that has barely anything to do with the anthropological reality of male-female coupling.

Does this matter? The Church, among many others, believes it does. If marriage were not a public institution — if the state were to cease to give legal recognition to marriage of any kind, making it a private matter — the discussion would not arise. But as the political philosopher Michael Sandel notes in his book *Justice*, "the case for same-sex marriage can't be made on non-judgmental grounds. It depends on a certain conception of the *telos* of marriage — its purpose or point." As long as the state recog-nises marriage — conferring privileges and status on it — there needs to be debate about the virtues it honours and rewards, and the meaning of the institution, and the consequences of dethroning it in law. "The un-derlying moral question," Sandel says, "is unavoidable."

The discussion against same-sex marriage must begin with three questions: What is marriage for? Why should the state support it? And what happens when it is redefined?

✝ POSITIVE INTENTION

There are many positive values invoked by advocates of gay marriage, starting, of course, with those of equality and fairness. In principle, all are equal before the law, and minorities need the state's recognition and protection. Marriage is about commitment and love; which state and society should be encouraging.

The Purpose of Marriage

Marriage has never been 'equal' in the sense of allowing anyone to enter it under any circumstances; loving a person does not give you the legal right to marry them unless you fulfil the requirements designed to protect the goods for which the institution exists. Thus, a man cannot marry a woman who is already married; nor can a woman who loves two men marry them both. We cannot, in the name of equality, allow all those who love each other to marry, unless, of course, we were to agree that marriage means nothing at all. Nor does same-sex marriage create equal access to marriage: It restricts marriage to two people rather than three or more, and it does not allow same-sex relatives to marry. Same-sex marriage, in other words, does not open marriage to all; it continues to discriminate against whole swathes of people who remain ineligible. Indeed, given the low take-up of same-sex marriage (a point we'll come to later), it has barely increased access to marriage at all.

What happens with same-sex marriage is that the law replaces one notion of marriage with a radically different one, one that is thin and meaningless. The Church's objection to same-sex marriage has nothing to do with its view of homosexuality (see Chapter 2), but concerns rather this new understanding of marriage.

Until relatively recently, the Church and the state's understanding of marriage was very similar. Marriage is a natural institution that precedes both Church and state and has been recognised and promoted by both for the same reason: that it is a conjugal institution that benefits both those involved and their offspring. In almost all cultures and ages, marriage is seen as encouraging heterosexual bonding, bringing men and women together for life for the raising of children by their natural parents in a framework of permanence and stability, something of overriding importance to all human societies in all places and at all times.

The Church has always supported and promoted marriage for all these reasons. It has, in addition, a theological understanding of marriage as a vehicle of God's grace, which is why the Church considers it a sacrament. But it only holds its own members — the baptised — to that understanding. When Catholics argue against redefining marriage in law, they do so not in order to impose 'their' understanding of marriage, but as citizens concerned for defending the social goods of the institution.

Both Church and state provide access to marriage and regulate it; but neither Church nor state has the right to redefine it, because it belongs to society. Yet this is what public authorities in some 25 nations in the Western world have done. By choosing to recognise as 'marriage' a union of two people of the same sex, the state has explicitly rejected the conjugal understanding of marriage as a union of husband and wife for the primary task of begetting and nurturing children. As Bishop Denis Nulty of Kildare & Leighlin wrote in a 2015 pastoral letter:

> "We cannot teach future generations that preparing yourself for planning a family based on the stable relationship between a man and a woman is the same as living with a person of the same sex. Let us also be aware that, in seeking to advance a supposed claim on behalf of the rights of adults, we may be setting aside the far greater right of children (who are the only ones who should be privileged in this situation) to rely on models of father and mother, mum and dad."

The Church believes the state should continue to promote conjugal marriage, not because it disapproves of gay people or rejects any particular group in society, but because of what it believes about marriage, family, and children, namely:

1. The family is the founding unit of civil society, the vital building block on which human society is built;

2. at the heart of the family is the sexual union of a man and a woman given to each other for their sake and for the good of their children; and

3. conjugal marriage provides the ideal, irreplaceable environment for the raising of children, who benefit psychologically, emotionally, and in countless other ways from it; and that is why it should be advocated and encouraged by the state.

Necessary Discrimination

"To affirm heterosexuality as a requirement for marriage is not to discriminate," wrote Cardinal Jorge Mario Bergoglio, the future Pope Francis, when he was Archbishop of Buenos Aires in 2010, "but to start from an objective fact...Marriage is founded on the complementary union of a man and a woman, whose natures are enriched by what this radical diversity brings." This understanding of marriage implies that some are excluded from it — not least those who wish to marry others of the same sex. There is nothing unjustly discriminatory in relying on genuinely relevant distinctions. Equality is not equivalence. A pension provision designed to improve the lot of the elderly necessarily excludes the young. A tax break for a company that sets up in a deprived area excludes all those that don't (and so on).

States and churches have always imposed restrictions on marriage, where these are reasonable, in order to support the nature and meaning of the institution and the goods for which it exists. Thus same-sex couples have not before now been able to access marriage because marriage is a procreative institution; nor can relatives (because of the genetic problems of consanguinity), nor people with psychological or physical impediments, because those entering marriage need to be capable of understanding its obligations and assuming them — which excludes those under-age or not of sound mind. Others are excluded from marriage for other reasons: you cannot marry if you are already married, you cannot marry more than one person, and you cannot marry unless you agree to remain married on a permanent basis. The exclusions are not arbitrary: traditionally marriage has excluded bigamous and same-sex unions, as well as open, temporary, polyamorous, and polyandrous unions, in order to protect the meaning of the institution.

In summary, marriage exists and is promoted for three essential reasons: to encourage the birth and upbringing of children, to provide the best possible setting for children to grow up in and to ensure the cooperation of men and women for the common good.

Those reasons tell us about the intrinsic nature of marriage. Living together in a committed relationship is not a sufficient criterion. Nor is being sexually involved. Rearing children together is not enough to make a marriage. Equally, same-sex partnerships, whatever their moral status, cannot be marriages because they lack an essential orientation to children; even when a sexual act is involved, it cannot be generative.

The Catholic argument against same-sex marriage is not, essentially, religious but is made from reason and natural law. Marriage is a public social institution, singled out and promoted by state, faith and civil society, because it serves a far-reaching social good. Every child that has ever been born has been created by a mother and a father, and every society has always regarded this fact as of such significance that marriage — the institution which brings together a man and a woman to provide a place of nurture for that child — has been elevated to the status of a social institution. The Church believes that the state should remain committed to the conjugal understanding of marriage because law teaches culture. The stability of male-female partnerships raising children is, in fact, the sole reason for the state taking an interest in and supporting marriage. Loving relationships are not otherwise the business of the state. As Bishop of Elphin Dr Kevin Doran wrote in 2015: "It is true, of course, that all people are equal. Reason, however, points to the truth about human sexuality that makes the relationship of man and woman unique. This uniqueness has been recognised in every culture and has always been associated with the openness of marriage to the gift of life. That is why society has always sought to guard with special care the institution of marriage. Why would we suddenly want to change that now?" If there are injustices against people in relationships other than marriage, the Church believes that those injustices can certainly be reformed and corrected in other ways rather than redefining marriage. Bishop Doran added: "we need to acknowledge that the issue of same sex-relationship is a reality for many in our society and, among them, families in our own parishes. We need to remember that we are 'all called into one and the same hope' (Ephesians 4:4). This is a challenge for the Church, both now and for the years ahead."

If marriage is no longer defined as conjugal, the state no longer has a reason to promote it. The reason for promoting it — to encourage the biological union of man and woman, which gives rise to the best possible environment for children — has disappeared. What happens, then, to the children?

Who Cares about the Kids?

A conjugal relationship is much more than a sexual relationship; it is a sexual relationship that by its nature — not automatically and not always, because children are a gift, but generally and normatively — produces children. Even when a married couple cannot have children, they are still capable of offering a child a home with a mother and a father. The fact that a particular couple cannot have children — because of age or the heartbreak of infertility — does not alter the fact that men and women are by nature capable of doing so. When the law restricts marriage to a man plus a woman, it is recognising that fact.

By upholding conjugal marriage, the state recognises that children raised by their biological parents are in a uniquely beneficial position. All things being equal, children fare best when raised by their own parents in a context of permanence and stability. It is in the interest of society as a whole that as many children as possible are raised in this way, which is why government social policy has traditionally been to encourage this outcome by all possible means. Same-sex marriage sends the opposite message: Children do not need a mum and a dad, and if the 'products' of one's sperm and egg are not necessarily one's own children, why does sex and childbearing need to take place within marriage? Same-sex 'marriage' eliminates in law and weakens in culture the ideal that children should be conceived, born and raised by their married, natural parents.

Of course, marriage does not exist solely for children, and people do not marry solely for the purpose of having children. There are many social goods which marriage encourages — commitment, fidelity and stability, for example. But these are firstly goods for children, and the reason the state promotes marriage is because marriage is best for children. As endless studies demonstrate, children in low-conflict married homes are less likely to suffer child poverty, sexual and physical abuse, or mental or physical ill-health; they also are less likely to misuse drugs, commit crimes, suffer disadvantage in the workplace or become divorced and un-married parents themselves.

The weight of social-science evidence strongly supports the idea that family structure matters and that children do best when raised by their own mother and father in a stable, low-conflict marriage. It is not simply the presence of two parents, but the presence of two *biological* parents, that best supports children's development. That's why the state pro-motes marriage by singling it out in law. "Marriage brings not only clear economic benefits but social benefits as well, enabling children to grow up to be more successful than they might otherwise be," as Ron Haskins and Isabel Sawhill put in a 2004 Brookings Institute book, *Creating an Opportunity Society*. "To those who argue that this goal [of promoting marriage] is old-fashioned or inconsistent with modern culture, we argue that modern culture is inconsistent with the needs of children."

Some object that the reality is now very different: that marriage has in fact broken down to the point where, in some areas, there are at least as many children born out of wedlock as within it, and so for the state to promote marriage is an attempt to close the stable door after the horse has bolted. But this is an argument for the state getting out of marriage altogether, not for weakening it by redefining it as a mere partnership. And it is not the argument made by governments introducing same-sex marriage, who have argued in favour of strengthening marriage.

Some same-sex marriage advocates, accepting the premise that mar-riage benefits children, point to children now being raised by same-sex couples; marriage, they claim, is needed to protect them. But children are raised in many different ways; that is not an argument for changing marriage. When the state promotes (conjugal) marriage as uniquely ben-eficial for children, it is not declaring official disapproval of the myriad other ways children are being brought up in the less-than-ideal circum-stances, often with great love and care, by single parents, divorced par-ents, step-parents, aunts and uncles and same-sex couples. Sometimes these arrangements are saving children from a much worse fate; it might be better for a child to be brought up by a same-sex couple than to remain, for example, in an orphanage. But at the same time, it would be foolish to deny that in all these cases children are deprived of something they need for a healthy psychological upbringing. The law upholds what is in the best interest of children. What is in their best interest is not a same-sex couple, or a single parent, or divorced parents — however loving these may be. Some same-sex marriage advocates even claim that mothers or fathers are disposable in the life of a child — but no one believes that to be true when there's abandonment, divorce or the death of a parent, all of which leave a gap in a child's life.

Some cite studies attempting to show that children raised by same-sex couples fare just as well as those raised by a mother and father. Almost all of these studies are extremely limited in scope, based on self-selecting samples, are not longitudinal — that is, do not track the welfare of children over time, and are based on minuscule numbers.

One piece of research based on solid data was that of American sociologist Paul Sullins, who surveyed 512 children with same-sex parents drawn from the US National Health Interview Survey. Writing in the February 2015 *British Journal of Education, Society & Behavioural Science*, a peer-reviewed journal, Sullins concludes that children's "emotional problems [are] over twice as prevalent for children with same-sex parents than for children with opposite-sex parents" and included misbehaviour, worrying, depression, poor relationships with peers and inability to concentrate. "It is no longer accurate," concludes Sullins, "to claim that no study has found children in same-sex families to be disadvantaged relative to those in opposite-sex families." Sullins found evidence for what is obvious to most people: that opposite-sex parents provide a better environment for children. "Biological parentage uniquely and powerfully distinguishes child outcomes between children with opposite-sex parents and those with same-sex parents," he writes. "The primary benefit of marriage for children, therefore, may not be that it tends to present them with improved parents (more stable, financially affluent, etc., although it does this), but that it presents them *with their own* parents."

To love a child is one thing; to love a child with a love that provides the necessary structure is another. The child needs a clear and coherent genealogy. In the case of a single parent, the child yearns for the missing mother or father. In the case of a same-sex couple, children are deprived of the chance to relate equally well to the other sex. It is not the sexual *orientation* of the people bringing up a child that is relevant to that child's wellbeing, but their sexual *complementarity*. To be a father or a mother is not merely an affective, cultural, or social function; parenting involves sexual difference.

In a February 2015 open letter to US Supreme Court Justice Anthony Kennedy, the adult child of a loving lesbian couple insisted that the rights of children must trump the feelings of adults. "The adults in this scenario," wrote Katy Faust, "satisfy their heart's desires, while the child bears the most significant cost: missing out on one or more of her biological parents. Making policy that intentionally deprives children of their fundamental rights is something that we should not endorse, incentivise, or promote." She added: "We are made to know, and be known by, both of our parents. When one is absent, that absence leaves a lifelong gaping wound." As the French rabbi Gilles Bernheim puts it:

> "The child is not an object of rights but a subject of rights. To speak of a 'right to a child' instrumentalises and objectifies the child. In the current debate, the child as a person, as a subject, is absent in the arguments of those who demand adoption for homosexual couples. This absence allows adults demanding rights to avoid asking about the rights of the child, what the child might need, and whether the child might prefer having a father and mother instead of two parents of the same sex. This is a case where our carelessness borders on cynicism. The right of the child is radically different from the right to the child. The former right is fundamental. It consists in particular in giving the child a family in which he will have the best chance to have the best life."

What It Means to Abandon the Meaning of Marriage

One of the surprising facts about gay marriage — given how it is framed as a long-suppressed civil right — is how few gay people actually enter it. Despite the stream of news coverage of those first couples who avail themselves of the legal recognition in various countries and states when same-sex marriage first becomes available, the take-up has been universally small. In Ireland, in the twelve months following the introduction of same-sex marriage just 1,082 couples availed of marriage. In 2016, the number was 1,147. In the Netherlands, the first country to legalise same-sex marriage, just 12% of same-sex cohabiting couples had married by 2005, compared with 82% of heterosexual couples. In Spain, a country of 46 million inhabitants, there are about 3,100 homosexual marriages each year, after an initial 4,300 of these marriages in 2006, the year after homosexual marriage was made legal there. In the UK, a nation of 60 million, just 1,400 same-sex couples rushed to tie the knot in the months after marriage redefinition came into effect in 2014. In Canada, there are just 21,000 married same-sex couples out of 6.29 million total married couples.

But do same-sex marriages, despite their low numbers, give a particularly fine example of longevity and commitment? The evidence here is all the other way. In the Netherlands and Belgium, the divorce rate among same-sex couples is far higher than among couples as a whole. Belgium is particularly striking: male same-sex couples are 21% more likely to divorce than heterosexual couples, while lesbian married couples are an amazing 76% more likely to divorce. The instability of woman-woman relationships has long been recorded in the figures: in Norway and Sweden the risk of breakups for female same-sex partnerships more than doubles that found in male unions; in the UK, lesbian relationships make up 44% of same-sex civil partnerships but 62% of dissolutions, while in Sweden 30% of female same-sex marriages are likely to end in divorce within six years of formation, compared with 20% for male same-sex marriages and 13% for heterosexual marriages.

But given that the take-up of gay marriage is so low, surely the instability of same-sex relationships will not affect the institution of marriage overall?

It is assumed by many that same-sex marriage can exist alongside traditional, heterosexual marriage almost as a parallel institution, or as a small subset of marriage. But society takes its cue from cultural norms, which are partly reflected in, and partly shaped by, the law. In redefining marriage, the law teaches that marriage is concerned with emotional and sexual unions rather than biological union or children. Because there is no reason why friendship should be permanent, exclusive, or limited to two, same-sex marriage means that the traditional marriage norms of permanence, exclusivity and monogamy make little sense. Gay marriage doesn't lead automatically to demands for the legalisation of polygamous or polyamorous unions, but it makes it much harder to argue against them. For having abandoned a conjugal conception of marriage, and replaced it with a conception of marriage that has adult companionship as its focus, there is no principled basis for resisting the extension of marriage licences to polygamist and polyamorist unions. In the Netherlands and Brazil, there have been demands for the legal recognition of three-way unions, and in Canada proposals for temporary unions. As Sherif Girgis, Ryan T. Anderson, and Robert P. George show in their book *What is Marriage? Man and Woman: A Defence*, the redefinition of marriage makes it harder, over time, to live by marriage's norms and to urge them on others. Same-sex marriage appears to create more marriage; but over time, it creates far less marriage.

The main effect is to accelerate the decline of marriage and family; fewer children will be raised by their natural parents, and the state will need to play an even larger role in their health, education and welfare. Same-sex marriage thereby consolidates and accentuates the destruction of the traditional family as a social institution that brings together friendship, companionship, emotional kinship and love, the begetting of children and their protection and care, and their early education and induction into an identity and a history. Same-sex marriage means that almost everything that marriage once brought together has now been split apart. Sex has been divorced from marriage, marriage from procreation, and having children from biologically generating them. These trends were already evident before same-sex marriage, as result of in vitro fertilisation, birth control and the ethics of autonomy, but same-sex marriage endorses and consolidates the trends.

The result is a new form of poverty, and a divide within society the likes of which have not been seen since the nineteenth century. Those who are privileged to grow up in stable loving association with the two people who brought them into being will, on average, be healthier physically and emotionally, will do better at school and at work and will have more successful relationships, be happier and live longer.

Sarah Teather, a Catholic former member of the British Parliament and passionate advocate of equality and social justice, defied her Liberal

Democrat party and the government when she voted against same-sex marriage in 2013.

> "We know that permanent stable loving relationships between parents are very important for children. Such relationships make it much easier to offer the kind of consistent loving parenting that enables children to grow into healthy, happy adults able to play their part in society...[but] by moving to a definition of marriage that no longer requires sexual difference, we will, over time, ultimately decouple the definition of marriage from family life altogether. I doubt that this change will be immediate. It will be gradual, as perceptions of what marriage is and is for shift. But we can already see the foundations for this shift in the debate about same-sex marriage...Once the concept of marriage has become established in social consciousness as an entirely private matter about love and commitment alone, without any link to family, I fear that it will accelerate changes already occurring that makes family life more unstable."

A second effect is the way that advocacy of the traditional view of marriage comes to be seen as coterminous with bigotry and intolerance. Once it becomes the official policy of the state and public institutions that it does not matter whether a child is the offspring of a biological union of mother and father or whether he or she is brought up by a same-sex couple — in Spain, birth certificates have been amended to say 'Progenitor A' and 'Progenitor B' — no kind of arrangement for bringing up children can be proposed as an ideal, and to suggest otherwise is 'discriminatory' and evidence of 'bigotry'.

Once the new, 'tolerant' definition of marriage becomes the state's official position, to be accepted by all public employees, dissenting individuals and organisations face anti-discrimination lawsuits or the withdrawal of public funds. In a 2012 article for *National Review*, Michael Coren records how, in Canada, "it is estimated that, in less than five years, there have been between 200 and 300 proceedings — in courts, human-rights commissions, and employment boards — against critics and opponents of same-sex marriage. And this estimate doesn't take into account the casual dismissals that surely have occurred." From the wedding-cake baker to the florist to the schoolteacher, even in a Catholic school espousing Church teaching, these clashes with the new orthodoxy are multiplying in the US.

Public law and policy will increasingly come to reflect an eviscerated, weak narrative of marriage involving mere domestic partnership. By reducing the significance of marriage in the eyes of society, by rendering marriage less distinct and important, same-sex marriage makes it even harder for future generations to see the point of marriage. It puts marriage on an unstable juridical foundation, making it hard to see why, if one essential element of marriage has been stripped out, the other elements should remain as well. And it makes it much harder, over time, for children to be raised as they justly deserve to be — by a mother and a father in a stable, committed, sexually exclusive relationship.

■ EXISTING FRAME

Gay marriage is simply the latest chapter in the emancipation of gay people. Allowing gay people to marry is an issue of basic equality, and those who oppose their right to do so are in favour of discrimination. The Church disapproves of gay people and naturally opposes gay marriage, but what right do Christians have to dictate our laws? Gay people nowadays enter into committed, loving relationships, and many of them bring up children. Why shouldn't they be given the chance for the legitimacy and social approval that marriage brings? Why should they be second-class citizens?

↺ REFRAME

Discrimination against gay people is wrong, but it cannot be addressed by overthrowing the conjugal meaning of marriage in law. This is a question about what marriage means and whether the state should support that meaning. The state has upheld and promoted marriage because of its unique and irreplaceable benefits for children, and for society as a whole, when they are raised by their biological parents. If the state now redefines marriage so that it is no longer about a man and a woman but rather a mere partnership, then the state is no longer promoting marriage and is in practice undermining it. The public meaning and purpose of marriage is eliminated, marriage comes to be seen as simply a relationship of consenting adults, and parenthood comes to be understood solely as a legal phenomenon of those choosing to take responsibility for a child. The social function marriage plays in society — providing children with their natural mother and father — would be lost. The Church does not seek to impose a theological view of marriage; it respects civil marriage. But it cannot be silent when the interests of children and the common good of society are discarded under the false pretext of overcoming discrimination.

★ KEY MESSAGES

- ▶ The demand for same-sex marriage is not a demand for marriage to be extended to gay people but for marriage to be redefined so that it is no longer linked to the begetting and raising of children by their natural parents. In turning marriage into a mere partnership, the law renders marriage largely meaningless and makes it less likely that children will be raised in ways that best suit them.

- ▶ The slogan 'equal marriage' implies equality of access to the same institution; but in fact, it means overthrowing the institution, making marriage equal to non-marital relationships.

- ▶ The Church believes the state should continue to promote conjugal marriage, not because it disapproves of gay people or rejects any particular group in society, but because it believes marriage is a conjugal institution that the state should promote and protect for the sake of society and above all of children.

- ▶ Same-sex marriage enshrines in law the idea that the gender is incidental to marriage and the raising of children, such that all those who believe otherwise become vulnerable to the accusation that they are promoting discrimination and prejudice.

Chapter 6

Defending the Unborn in a Throwaway Culture

Challenging Questions

- Why would the Catholic Church want abortion to be illegal? Shouldn't a woman have the right to choose?
- Why does the Church put its dogma before the medical benefits of embryonic research?
- Why would the Church crush the hopes of infertile couples wanting to have a child by opposing IVF and surrogacy?
- Who is going to help a woman in a difficult situation?

Ever since abortion was framed as a question of autonomy — a woman's 'right to choose' — and snagged in debates about civil rights, the debate over its legality has become one of the most neuralgic in contemporary Western culture and the source of tremendous pain and confusion. In the United States alone, there have been upwards of 58 million abortions since the Supreme Court in 1973 legalised abortion during all three trimesters of a pregnancy. Since the 1967 Abortion Act in the UK, more than 8.8 million unborn children have lost their lives. Today, one in five pregnancies in Britain ends in abortion. Yet because it continues to be framed as an individual, private matter, the impact on society of the vast scale of this lawful, intended death has barely been discussed — and seldom with civility.

The Catholic Church's defence of unborn lives is probably its best-known public position, the vigorous advocacy of a right to human life that much of contemporary society fails to recognise. The Church cares not just about abortion, but about unborn human life wherever it is experimented on, cloned, created and killed — treated as a mere 'bunch of cells' instead of a God-created early human life deserving of respect.

As Bishop of Elphin Kevin Doran wrote in a February 2018 pastoral letter on the Church's consistent pro-life ethic:

> "When it comes to the right to choose, there is a tendency to forget that there is another person involved, a vulnerable person who has no choice and who depends entirely on others for protection. If society accepts that one human being has the right to end the life of another, then it is no longer possible to claim the right to life as a fundamental human right for anybody. A number of EU member states have already legalised euthanasia. I am convinced that if we concede any ground on abortion, the very same arguments which are now being used to justify abortion will be used to justify ending the lives of frail elderly people and people with significant disability. This is the final frontier. If we cross it, there will be no easy way back."

Despite occasional and incremental victories in what has become an ecumenical civil rights movement, the culture of death that Pope St John Paul II warned about in his encyclical *Evangelium Vitae* has come to pass. As Cardinal Timothy Dolan of New York observed in 2014:

> "When reason takes over, nobody prefers abortion. We see it as a tragedy to be avoided. But, unfortunately reason has been deluded here, because of the power of the abortion culture. And yes, what we have now, sadly, is that sometimes abortion is preferred, and sometimes abortion is even — in the twisted culture that we've got — thought to be virtuous. Sometimes abortion is thought to be the right choice. All you have to do is talk with brave women — and brave fathers — who carry a baby in their womb who has been diagnosed with Down Syndrome. They will tell you about the pressure they feel to abort the baby. They'll tell you about the people who tell them that it would be virtuous to abort the baby. What we've got now is a culture where sometimes abortion is preferred. Abortion is pushed. Abortion is advocated. And there are some people who would like to see abortion even mandated — as it is in China."

Catholics understandably feel powerless to forestall what can seem like an inexorable slide into the dehumanisation of the unborn, and are frustrated when they are unjustly framed as opponents of 'women's rights'. It can often seem as if the prophetic voice pointing to the humanity of the silent unborn victim — whether the 12- or 20-week-old baby destroyed by suction methods or the cluster of human cells in the petri dish, a complete human being in its early stage — is simply ignored by a society that thinks it too disturbing. Placing an absolute value on autonomy or the possibility of a cure, society seems to be growing more, not less, deaf to cries on behalf of the voiceless victims.

Yet the direction of Western cultural history, indelibly marked by Christianity, is toward the eventual revelation of the humanity of the victim. Just as the voices of the slave, the ostracised foreigner, the wife subjected to domestic violence, those with a disability, and the abused child have all, eventually, been heard, so will, eventually, the voice of the literally voiceless — the unborn.

There are some signs that Western society is beginning to awaken from that deafness. In Italy, where abortion became legal in 1978, seven out of ten gynaecologists now refuse to perform abortions – up from 59% in 2005. Many young doctors are refusing to participate in abortions and are exercising their right to conscientiously object.

In the US, survey after survey reveals rising discomfort at the prevalence and frequency of abortion and the price that has been paid since legalisation in 1973. Empathy with the embryo — rather than the 10-week-old child in the womb — is not yet apparent to the same degree. But it is a matter of time. "We've wandered in the desert for 40 years, but we're getting closer to the Promised Land," Cardinal Seán O'Malley of Boston told the National Prayer Vigil for Life in Washington, DC, in January 2013. "Younger Americans are more pro-life than ever." A 2010 Gallup survey found that "support for making abortion broadly illegal (was) growing fastest among young adults," and that this represented "a sharp change from the late 1970s, when seniors were substantially more likely than younger age groups to want abortion to be illegal".

Polls show that 75% of Americans know that despite the euphemisms surrounding it, abortion is the taking of human life. The key is to shift public opinion away from the common belief that abortion is a necessary evil.

This has happened with another pro-life campaign spearheaded by the Church in the face of often hostile public opinion. Catholics in the 1990s used to support capital punishment by about the same percentage (68%, according to a CBS poll) as the general public, but Mass-going Catholics are now more likely (56% according to a recent Zogby poll) than the general population to oppose it. The fall in overall support for the death penalty (to 66%, according to Gallup) shows that the Church's witness can be ahead of opinion.

Pope Francis is the master reframer in pointing to the unborn child as a victim of a broader 'throwaway' culture. In a speech to the International Federation of Catholic Medical Associations in the autumn of 2013, he identified "a widespread utilitarian mentality that now enslaves the hearts and minds of many" that "requires the elimination of human beings, especially if they are physically or socially weaker". He added:

> "Every child who, rather than being born, is condemned unjustly to being aborted, bears the face of Jesus Christ, bears the face of the Lord, who even before he was born, and then just after birth, experienced the world's rejection. And every elderly person — I spoke of children: let us move to the elderly, another point! And every elderly person, even if he is ill or at the end of his days, bears the face of Christ. They cannot be discarded, as the throwaway culture suggests! They cannot be thrown away!"

In April 2014, he showed how the victims are not just the unborn children but also their mothers. "Abortion compounds the grief of many women," said Francis, "who now carry with them deep physical and spiritual wounds after succumbing to the pressures of a secular culture which devalues God's gift of sexuality and the right to life of the unborn."

In the defence of innocent unborn life, no one should feel obliged to assert the 'rights' of the embryo against the 'rights' of adult human beings, as if this were a question of competing claims in a utilitarian calculation. Abortion degrades all those who take part in it. It is never a solution. It is a shameful thing for any society to collude in, one which is justified by a false notion of autonomy.

In opposing abortion, Catholics are not opposing progress, or women's rights or equality, but rather the reverse. They are like the anti-slave trade campaigners in the first years of the nineteenth century, hopeful that, however long it may take, society will eventually wake up to the humanity of the unborn. "In the history of our country, people of faith have worked together to overcome racism and injustice," Cardinal O'Malley said at the same 2013 rally. "Now we come together to be the defence attorney for the innocent unborn and the vulnerable elderly and all those whose right to life is threatened. We shall overcome."

✝ POSITIVE INTENTION

Abby Johnson, the abortion clinic director turned pro-life campaigner, says in her book *UnPlanned* that she "had never been interested in promoting abortion." She explains:

"I'd come to Planned Parenthood eight years before, believing that its purpose was primarily to prevent unwanted pregnancies, thereby reducing the number of abortions. That had certainly been my goal. And I believed that Planned Parenthood saved lives — the lives of women who, without the services provided by this organisation, might resort to some back-alley butcher."

Most advocates of legal abortion justify it as a necessary sacrifice for a greater good — usually the woman herself, who might otherwise be trapped in a loveless relationship, forced into the hands of back-street abortionist, or lose control over her life. The value behind arguments for legal abortion is almost always compassion, as it is for those who back embryonic stem-cell research on the grounds that it may lead to cures.

Life from the Start

The Church's consistent opposition to abortion is anchored in its reflection on Scripture. In the Old Testament, Exodus and the Psalms, among other books, reveal a God who knows His creatures even before they are born, and who forms, names, and loves the child in the womb. At the heart of the Church's advocacy is this knowledge of God as the author of our being. As the Congregation for the Doctrine of the Faith (CDF) summarised in the 1987 document *Donum Vitae*: "Human life is sacred because from its beginning it involves 'the creative action of God' and it remains forever in a special relationship with the Creator, who is its sole end. God alone is the Lord of life from its beginning until its end: No one can, in any circumstance, claim for himself the right to destroy directly an innocent human being." Hence the Second Vatican Council's description of abortion and infanticide as "abominable crimes".

Yet abortion is not a religious question but a matter of human rights. You do not need to believe that God is the author of life in order to observe that life begins in the womb; scan technology makes it possible for anyone to see for themselves. "Anyone who has ever seen a sonogram or has spent even an hour with a textbook on embryology knows that emotions are not the deciding factor [in abortions]," wrote Christopher Hitchens, the crusading left-wing atheist in his column for the *Nation* magazine in April 1989. "In order to terminate a pregnancy, you have to still a heartbeat, switch off a developing brain…break some bones and rupture some organs." It amazed Hitchens, whose anti-abortion stance made him unpopular in progressive circles, how the "majority of feminists and their allies have stuck to the dead ground of 'Me Decade' possessive individualism, an ideology that has more in common than it admits with the prehistoric right, which it claims to oppose but has in fact encouraged."

Abby Johnson, who had two abortions and worked enthusiastically for an abortion clinic until experiencing an awakening, says: "I didn't get into the industry because I was an atheist. I firmly believed in God. I believed I was empowering women to do what they needed." The slave traders, too, believed in God. But their consciences had dulled; they needed a conversion in order — like John Newton, creator of the 'Amazing Grace' hymn — to begin to treat their slaves as people and eventually to advocate an end to the trade. When Johnson was told to double the number of abortions each month, the scales began to fall from her eyes. She was not part of a charity, but a corporation concerned with making money that had commodified human life. She began to rebel. Now she works in a pro-life ministry that aims for the conversion of those working inside the abortion industry.

The slave traders knew that the slaves were human beings like them, but suppressed the knowledge of that fact by referring to them with contempt and treating them worse than animals. Similarly, pro-abortionists refer to a woman's 'right to choose what to do with her body' and compare what grows inside a woman to a 'clump of cells' or a 'blob of protoplasm'. But language cannot create a new reality. A baby isn't part of a woman's body. An unborn baby is a baby. It cannot be compared to an appendix, a kidney or a set of tonsils. It is a separate new life, entrusted to her to nurture. The question is what value — morally, socially and legally — the life has.

The notion that every human life is intrinsically precious, and not of greater or lesser value according to its stage of development (or other characteristics), is not just an article of Christian religious faith but a basic tenet of human-rights doctrine underpinning Western society. To claim that some living human beings do not deserve respect or should not be treated as 'persons' (based on changeable factors such as age, condition, location, or lack of mental or physical abilities) is to deny the very idea of inherent human rights. What the Catholic Church teaches, that human life is not of lesser value when it is younger and less developed, is the foundational principle of democracy. The alternative has only ever been sustained by totalitarian regimes and racist ideologies.

Abortion as Eugenics

The abortion question, then, is really two questions: the wrongness/licitness of abortion itself, and what the law and the state should determine.

Few dare to argue that abortion is a moral good, although there are those who try to sustain that it is a matter of indifference. But there is an argument based on the moral strength of autonomy: women, as those responsible for the upbringing of a child, have the right to determine for themselves whether to give birth or interrupt their pregnancy. But this argument can only be considered if abortion is a morally neutral action, or a moral right; yet there is no moral right to abortion, just as there is no right to own other human beings or to rape another person. Laws against abortion, slavery, rape and murder may restrict the autonomy of others, but they are not a restriction on their freedom; the law recognises no freedom to harm others.

The other argument is a pragmatic one. Given that unplanned pregnancies are inevitable, and that some women will always seek to end them, those who do so should not be criminalised and the activity should be regulated and supervised. Yet this argument, too, depends on seeing it as a morally inconsequential act. The widespread occurrence of rape should not lead one to advocate the repeal of laws against rape, and the rise of human trafficking in our time is not an argument for re-introducing slavery. The law cannot collaborate in or encourage the suffering or destruction of the vulnerable, lest it end up teaching society that what is deeply wrong is socially acceptable.

Those who advocate abortion always claim that it should be safe, egal and rare. But the experience is that where abortion is introduced, it becomes commonplace. There is also the fact that where abortion is permitted, it becomes a socially acceptable (even if seldom discussed) back-up to failed contraception. As Pope St John Paul II warned, it has led to "the supremacy of the strong over the weak". The decision to terminate a pregnancy is frequently made after learning that a baby is disabled, often in the doctor's office where a woman discovers a disability through a pre-natal scan. Medical staff will often suggest it at this point, and the abortion is carried out as a matter of routine; few will ever know. In this way, the termination of those society deems unfit or burdensome is being carried out daily, on a very large scale, yet silently — thus fulfilling, by a series of individual choices, the ambitions of the early twentieth-century eugenicists. In Britain, for example, 90% of unborn children diagnosed in the womb with Down Syndrome are now aborted. In Iceland, as of 2017, 100% of unborn children diagnosed with the syndrome were terminated – it is a pattern replicated in many Western countries.

Abortion was one of the methods the eugenicists wanted to use to reduce the 'rising tide of colour' in America's streets. Margaret Sanger, who founded Planned Parenthood in a two-room shack in the Brownsville section of Brooklyn in 1923, remains a hero to the abortion movement and her organisation one of the main providers of abortion in America. In *Pivot of Civilisation*, she described her objectives: "More children from the fit, less from the unfit — that is the chief aim of birth control." The people Sanger considered unfit were "all non-Aryan people" belonging to what she called the "dysgenic races" (Eastern Europeans and black people). Sanger believed that this "great biological menace to the future of civilisation...deserved to be treated like criminals" and proposed to "segregate morons who are increasing and multiplying" in order to produce "a race of thoroughbreds".

Abortion, notes Dennis Sewell in *The Political Gene*, "has had a greater impact in reducing births among the economically disadvantaged than the middle class, and is proportionately more frequently carried out on women from racial minorities in the United States." Some 70% of the clinics operated by Planned Parenthood in the US are in black and Hispanic neighbourhoods. For every three black babies born, two are aborted.

This was confirmed by 2011 figures released by the New York City Department of Health — the first detailed statistics on abortions performed in the city. They showed that the postal codes with the highest abortion rates overwhelmingly were also minority neighbourhoods. Cardinal Dolan called the data "downright chilling", and took part in an ecumenical media campaign to remind New Yorkers of the churches' crisis-pregnancy resources. "New York does not deserve the gravestone 'Abortion capital of the world'," he said. "Our boast is the Statue of Liberty, not the Grim Reaper."

Decades after *Roe v. Wade* made it possible to achieve the ambition of eugenics in the US, can the state continue to sanction the massive disposal of innocent human life, when it is clear that the human beings disposed of are, in their overwhelming majority, disabled, poor, and dark-skinned? The choice for our age is simple: to travel down the road charted for us by the eugenicists of the twentieth century, or to take a stand in favour of the equality and dignity of all humanity.

As Empathy Increases, a Growing Schizophrenia

Unease over abortion is growing as result of science, which is revealing the wondrous humanity of the unborn child. Just as the lithographs of slaves stacked like cordwood in the holds of slave ships over time eroded the British slave trade, ultrasound technology showing detailed foetal anatomy is forcing society to honestly face the reality of abortion — and the contradictions endorsed by the law. Back in 1998, Dr Steve Calvin, a high-risk pregnancy specialist, wrote:

"In the last two and one-half decades our ability to obtain clear images of the foetus has expanded the concept of the foetus as a patient. For example, unborn babies can be treated with medications for irregular heartbeats and receive blood transfusions. Indeed, blood flow patterns in tiny blood vessels can be analysed using colour Doppler techniques. Increasingly, there are surgical procedures that can benefit an unborn baby. A frequent use of ultrasound is to evaluate the health of our unborn patients. In high-risk situations we recommend weekly ultrasound 'check-ups' that look for prenatal breathing movements and other activities. There is inescapable schizophrenia when modern medicine works under an ethical construct in which a foetus is a patient only when the mother has conferred this status on him or her. The trouble is that this status can be withdrawn. But how can one foetus at five months deserve abortion when an anaemic foetus of the same age can undergo a blood transfusion in the next room?"

The revelation of the humanity of the unborn has made a mockery of the legal basis of abortion, the upper limit for which has been traditionally determined by the idea of 'viability' — i.e., when life can be sustained outside the womb, independent of the mother.

'A woman's right to choose' is a slogan; it has never been endorsed as an absolute or unconditional right in any country. In most cases, the law accepts that unborn life has rights, but is unable to agree on the point at which those rights can be asserted at the expense of other rights. The use of 'scientific' ways of determining the limits of a woman's right is a way of keeping the peace in a society divided over the issue. Yet what the science indisputably reveals is what those not blinded by ideology already knew — that the life in the womb is deeply, marvellously, human.

The growing empathy with the unborn lies behind the gradual but growing reaction against the prevalence and ease of access to abortion. A 2009 Gallup poll, carried out every year since 1995, found for the first time that more Americans self-identified as 'pro-life' than 'pro-choice'. It also found that those who think all abortion should be illegal (23%) for the first time topped the number of those who think there should be no legal restrictions at all (22%). Since then, 'pro-life' has outpolled 'pro-choice' in five of nine Gallup polls taken. Other survey data, including surveys taken by the General Social Survey, which has done polling since the early 1970s, show consistent, durable, and significant increases in opposition to abortion, especially among young people: Millennials (aged 18–29) are more pro-life than any other age group.

Based on Marist Institute for Public Opinion polling commissioned by the Knights of Columbus since 2008, Carl Anderson in *Beyond a House Divided* argues that "we don't need to move the two polarised halves of the American population toward a compromise position on abortion; we need to start our conversation in the place where the overwhelming majority of Americans already stand". In a 2015 poll, 84% of Americans want restrictions on abortion — including seven in ten who identify as 'pro-choice'.

Embryo Research

In the arguments over federal funding for embryonic stem-cell research in the US that began in the mid-1990s it was repeatedly claimed that the creation and cloning of human embryos (creating human-animal hybrids) would enable cures for Alzheimer's, Parkinson's and other diseases. Those who opposed the legalisation of this new development because of its disrespect for human life were depicted as religious fanatics putting obstacles in the path of medical progress. Science, we were told, needed the greatest freedom for success; and the United States, already the world leader in stem-cell research, needed a law that would unfetter its research laboratories and so help usher in a new generation of seemingly astonishing cures.

For sufferers of those ailments, this was irresponsible hype and a cruel deception. Embryonic stem-cell research has resulted in no significant medical developments. There are no treatments derived from embryonic stem cells. On the other hand, there are literally dozens of treatments involving adult stem cells (extracted from bone marrow or placentas), which are entirely ethical. Stem-cell science is indeed at the cutting edge of medical research; there have been huge strides made in creating new organs from stem cells. Yet none of these has involved embryonic stem cells.

The demand for embryonic research comes from private medical research companies seeking funding, who dangle the possibility of breakthroughs to attract funding. The huge expansion of public funding for human embryonic stem-cell research in the US — estimated by the National Institutes of Health to be $128 million in 2011 — marked the triumph of a deeply troubling dogma: that scientific inquiry should be unfettered. This dogma replaces an important traditional principle: that tampering with human life for medical purposes requires a compelling ethical justification. The ethical duty society owes to human life requires a stringent scrutiny of claims of possible benefits. This ethical calculus — a reasoned examination of the ethics weighed against the anticipated benefits — conflicts with the medical research lobby's unreasonable claim to be free of any such calculus. Good science has always been accompanied by ethical standards. Ethics is good for science. Standards and trust are key.

It suits the advocates of embryonic research to frame its opponents as religious fanatics opposing the freedom of scientific inquiry ("Remember Galileo!"). But the ethical calculus is not a religious idea; advocates of good science have always upheld it as a vital principle. If the ends always justified the means, there can be no objection to the kind of experiments carried out by Nazi scientists on human beings.

Catholics are sometimes asked by sufferers of terminal diseases, "How can you sit there and oppose something that could make me better?" They have been sold a lie. In actuality, adult stem-cell research is far more likely to produce a cure for them than embryonic stem-cell research. The newspapers may be talking about breakthroughs from embryonic research but the scientific journals are not.

Yet it is not because embryonic research has failed to produce the much-hyped cures that it is wrong. The real reason is that a human embryo is in its first stage of life, and to use human life as the subject of experimentation is to desecrate that life.

Few would maintain the cluster of cells that makes up an embryo is morally equivalent to other clusters of cells — cancerous cells, say, or the embryo of a rat. If the embryo were so regarded, there would not have been such debate within the Presidential Commission for the Study of Bioethical Issues on whether funding should be expanded or not.

Assisted Reproductive Technologies

Since the birth of the first 'test-tube baby' in 1978, thousands of children have been born each year from surrogacy, where a woman agrees to carry another couple's child, and an even higher number of children born through anonymous gamete donation, where a child is born of no biological relation to one or both parents. Meanwhile, scientists in the United Kingdom and United States are pushing to allow for the creation of 'three-parent embryos' in order to create superior DNA. As Christopher White, associate director of Catholic Voices USA, wrote in *OSV Newsweekly*, "The children born as a result of these arrangements are brought into the world via methods that intentionally sever them from their biological parents. Unlike adoption, which the Church accepts and promotes as it aims to provide a home for children who already lack parents, conception through assisted reproductive technology is rejected by the Church for the ill effects that it has on both the couple aiming to conceive and the children created from these techniques."

Assisted reproductive technology (ART) replaces an act of self-giving love between a man and woman with a technical procedure in the laboratory, while the children born from anonymous sperm or egg donation grow up longing to know their biological mothers or fathers. The process puts a price tag on the value of human life and reduces conception to a mere contractual procedure. *Dignitas Personae* ('The Dignity of the Person'), the 2008 Vatican guidance on bioethical questions, notes that "the Church does not say 'no' to reproductive technologies to deny an infertile couple, but to promote the best possible conditions for a child to enter the world".

The whole process encourages a disregard for the preciousness of human life. In vitro fertilisation (IVF) creates surplus embryos that are then frozen, destroyed or used for medical experiments. It also encourages a eugenic view of life, for inherent in the technique is selecting an embryo for implantation in the womb. 'Saviour siblings' and other forms of embryo selection use the technique known as pre-implantation genetic diagnosis (PGD), in which embryos are selected on the basis of a particular gene. The same power allows for embryos to be selected (or screened) for particular characteristics: gender, hair colour and so on. The first is legal, the second not (yet); but increasingly it is being asked, 'Why not?'

If a woman can abort a child because it is the wrong sex, or coming at the wrong time in her life, why not select a child that fits with her requirements and her convenience? If the means are accepted, then the 'right to choose' becomes limitless.

But creating life according to a specification and discarding all others strikes at the heart of the core moral principle undergirding a civilised society — that you don't use anyone else just for your own purposes, or even for other people's purposes. A human person needs to be treated as an end in him or herself, not as a tool for another — even another's health. It is on this principle that we condemn rape, torture and blackmail, that we don't allow experiments on people's bodies or minds without their consent, and that we don't breed human individuals to create a pool of organs that could be transplanted to save the lives of others.

The Church here, too, stands against the commodification and degradation of human life, and for a human ecology that respects the integrity of creation.

Women Deserve Better

The Church is sometimes told that this is a 'women's issue', yet consistently more men than women favour abortion. Abortion divides the sexes far less than it increasingly divides women: conservative women are the most anti-abortion segment of the population, while liberal women are the most in favour of abortion rights. Forty years after Roe v. Wade, activists find themselves having to vigorously and repeatedly defend abortion when faced with evidence that younger women no longer necessarily see it as one of their fundamental rights and are sceptical about the claims that justified its legalisation: it has not reduced out-of-wedlock births, child abuse, or crime rates. Deprived of cogent social reasons in favour of abortion, its advocates have resorted to the autonomy argument. Yet the individualist rhetoric that accompanies this argument strikes many women as deeply unfeminine.

"It's time to face the facts," writes Elise Italiano, a volunteer with Catholic Voices USA. "The brand of feminism that promotes abortion as the key to our freedom does not help us flourish, preserve our dignity or protect us from evils. A society that is poised to overturn Roe must put in place the structures and support for pregnant women so that the 'choice' between life and abortion is no longer difficult, because life is the natural choice. It's time to rethink the feminist case for abortion. It's time to fight the real war on women."

Catholics need to not just argue against abortion, but to help heal its wounds. They must above all care for women in need, through pre-natal care, adoption and post-abortion counselling. Abortion hurts; that has been the experience of the Church through ministering to the women and families who are the living victims of abortion. Project Rachel offers post-abortion healing — primarily the mercy of God to those who feel condemned and ashamed. In 2011, Cardinal Dolan in New York reiterated a longstanding commitment: If you are pregnant and in need, the Church will help you – this is replicated by parishes and dioceses across the world and the Church works hard to reach out to women experiencing crisis pregnancies and to help women choose to keep their child even when they are being pressured to abort. Cura, the Catholic-run pregnancy counselling agency, provides support for mothers and fathers. Sometimes they are experiencing a crisis pregnancy, oftentimes it is just for reassurance. Cura also provides support for new mothers and for women after having an abortion.

Catholics stand with those experiencing an unplanned pregnancy. It is not enough to oppose abortion. You have to back life, in deeds as well as words, and work for a new culture that really welcomes life.

■ EXISTING FRAME

Legal abortion enshrines in law a woman's right to choose. Neither the Church nor the state has any right to dictate to a woman whether or not she can see through her pregnancy. Abortion is not killing: the foetus is a blob of cells. That's why most people in this country believe abortion should be safe and legal. If the Church were allowed to impose its religious view of this, there would be a return to back-alley abortions.

Similarly, research on embryos, which are just a cluster of cells and not viable, gives the hope of finding a cure for terrible diseases. If the Church were really pro-life, it wouldn't oppose the selection of an embryo that can give stem cells to save their brother or sister, or oppose assisted reproductive technologies that give hope to couples who have difficulty conceiving.

↻ REFRAME

Abortion is not a religious issue, but one of human rights, beginning with the most important right of all — the right to life. The Church raises its voice on behalf of the silent victims, just as it does on behalf of others whose dignity is not recognised in a 'throwaway' culture. The pro-lifers are the contemporary equivalent of the anti-slavery campaigners of the early nineteenth century, seeking to awaken society to the plight of the voiceless. There are signs of that awakening happening, especially among Millennials.

Abortion is creating a eugenic society, where those deemed less worthy to live are being silently, and legally, destroyed. The corrosive effect of this runs deep. Embryos are the early stage of human life; they are vulnerable and need protection from the law, yet they are used and discarded in laboratories and fertility clinics. The Church stands against the commodification and degradation of human life, and for a human ecology that respects the integrity of creation.

The anti-abortion argument is a big 'yes' to life, and justice, and offers real choices to women frightened of unplanned or unwanted pregnancies, helping to create a society where all life is welcomed and valued.

★ KEY MESSAGES

▸ Embryos are the early stage of human life; they are vulnerable and need protection from the law. The worth of human life is not linked to its appearance or size — because an embryo is tiny makes it no less a human life worthy of care and protection.

▸ There is a moral awakening in American society — a growing awareness of the wonder and beauty of unborn life. The Catholic Church speaks on behalf of the voiceless, defenceless embryo, just as it speaks on behalf of other 'silent' victims.

▸ The Church works to promote public awareness of the fragility and value of unborn life and to offer real choices to women frightened of unplanned or unwanted pregnancies. This is not a matter of the rights of women versus other rights, but of what is good for all involved: the woman and her baby, and society as a whole.

Chapter 7

Never Again: *The Legacy of Clerical Sex Abuse*

Challenging Questions

- Why does the United Nations claim as recently as February 2014 that "the Holy See has consistently placed the preservation of the reputation of the Church and the protection of the perpetrators above children's best interests"?

- How could the Church, which preaches a Gospel of mercy for the suffering, have so consistently ignored the cries of victims?

- Given the huge numbers of priest abusers, isn't it time to end the mandatory celibacy rule?

The sexual abuse of minors by priests in the 1970s–80s, the cover-up and evasion by Church authorities at the time, and the fallout since — in terms of the ongoing pain of survivors, excoriating media coverage and endless lawsuits — add up to one of the greatest crises in Church history, a scandal that never seems to be over. This is, above all, a story of betrayal: by predatory priests who exploited the innocence of their victims, violating the sacred trust of the priesthood, and leaving the Church exposed to shame and lawsuits; by bishops, who failed to protect their flocks and the Church; and by the Vatican, who proved tone-deaf at first to the cries of victims and the demands for action. There is almost no one who has not been left bruised by the scandal, which continues to reverberate. Not only are there hundreds of survivors of abuse who have been left shattered, but also ordinary Catholics, including the clergy, who are left shaking their heads at the diabolic ferocity of it all.

Media focus has been intense, incessant and unforgiving. Many Catholics feel that the Church has been singled out and excoriated in ways that amount to a kind of persecution, and they point to the distortions and myths that the coverage has created. Pope Francis spoke for many when, a month after an excoriating United Nations report in February 2014 painted a grotesquely distorted picture of the Church's handling of the issue, he gently pointed out that it was "perhaps the single public institution to have moved with transparency and responsibility" on this issue.

On the other hand, the relentless focus is understandable. Given the Western media's natural sympathy for victims and desire to hold institutions accountable, clerical sex abuse — involving cover up of crimes, deafness to the voice of victims, hypocritical sexual misconduct, and abuse of trust — was never going to be given an easy ride. Given the Church's dominance in Irish life post-independence, the focus is not surprising. It is an unconscious tribute to the Church that it would be held to a higher standard; after all, it teaches the Gospel, which is a polemic against idols and sacrificing the innocent on the altar of institutions. This is the light in which many view the issue of clerical sex abuse and the bishops' 'cover-up'.

The media's coverage of the clergy sexual abuse crisis can be seen then as an example of Christian values unconsciously retained by Western journalism and being used to judge the Church, which on this issue seems to have forgotten them. By failing to put victims first, as the Gospel demands, the Church handed the media and secular powers the moral entitlement to demand that it be changed. Without that scrutiny, the voice of the victims would not have been heard and vital reforms may not have happened — at least not as speedily, as Fr Timothy Radcliffe OP has pointed out often the media protests against the Church with good reason. "If the media had not stuck to their guns then maybe we would never have faced the issue of sexual abuse" he said. Cardinal Seán O'Malley of Boston said "the media helped make our Church safer for children by raising up the issue of clergy sexual abuse and forcing us to deal with it".

In 2012, at a Vatican summit on the issue, Cardinal William Levada (then head of the Congregation for the Doctrine of the Faith) praised the strong anti-abuse policies of the Church in Ireland, Canada, the United States, Brazil, Great Britain, France, Belgium, Germany, South Africa, Australia and New Zealand, noting: "In many cases, such response came only in the wake of the revelation of scandalous behaviour by priests in the public media."

Yet the coverage has left the world with a distorted picture: that the Catholic priesthood shelters high numbers of abusers, or that the Church is somehow behind the curve of the rest of society on the issue, neither of which is true. What is now needed is to tell the story of the Church's ongoing conversion and transformation, and its remarkable achievements in dealing with the issue, which have gone largely unreported, as well as the work still to be achieved. The other task is to refute the myths that have grown up around the issue: that celibacy or homosexuality causes abuse, that Church processes obstruct civil laws, that priest abusers are left unpunished or that the Church's goal is the protection of its own reputation.

The other story is the growing awareness of sexual abuse of children and young people as a major social issue and the revelations of widespread failure to deal with it. The 2002 Sexual Abuse and Violence in Ireland (SAVI) report is the most extensive piece of research of the prevalence of sexual abuse in Ireland. Greg Daly, a journalist and prolific number-cruncher with *The Irish Catholic* newspaper, has analysed the figures extensively. He points out that according to SAVI roughly 27% of Irish adults in 2001 had been the victims of child sexual abuse. Given that the adult population in the following year's census was 2,904,172, this means that there must have been around 780,000 adult survivors of child sexual abuse walking around Ireland, according to Daly. Over 48% of abuse survivors had never disclosed their experiences to anyone before being surveyed. Just under 52% of abuse survivors surveyed had previously told family, friends, or others of their experiences. Daly points out that only about 5% of abuse cases had at that point been reported to the Gardaí. Other countries show a depressingly similar picture. In the United Kingdom, the United States, Germany, Switzerland and Australia, studies consistently find that around 20% of women and around 8% percent of men suffered sexual abuse as children, mostly in the family. In the Church in those countries, abuse has become extremely rare, while it remains alarmingly high in society at large. According to Andrew Brown, an atheist writing in *The Guardian*, "during the 1990s a child in Sweden, possibly the most secularised country in Europe, was between 10 and 30 times more likely to be sexually assaulted than an American Catholic was by his priest."

These figures do not exculpate the Church's past failures, but they help reveal a new mission for the Church now: to assist institutions in particular, and society at large, in coming to terms with the scourge of sexual abuse of children in their midst, as the Church has been forced to do. Fr Robert Oliver, the then-Vatican prosecutor for sexual abuse crimes, told *The Irish Catholic* in a 2014 interview that:

> "The missionary spirit of Ireland could be very helpful to us in bringing other parts of the world to where Ireland is. It's very encouraging for me to come to Ireland and see the very effective work that has been and is being done...What I'm taking away with me is the fact that the good work which is being done here can be shared with the rest of the world...the phrase everyone is using is 'best practices' and Ireland has a lot of best practice in this field. The Church might even begin to take a role of leadership, certainly without any pride: we have to do so humbly, we have to do so in a way which recognises the real hurt that we've caused. Over the past 20 years in places like Ireland, the Church has done remarkable work to bring people together to see what is needed to respond effectively to this crime in our midst. Sexual abuse of children is an area that most people would prefer not to hear about; we've been forced to look at it. We can help others to see where abuse really happens, especially in the families. We have a role, you might even call it leadership where we can assist society as a partner to face this issue. More and more, the Church can be a mirror to the wider society forcing people to face the issue of abuse."

✝ POSITIVE INTENTION

The abuse of innocence, and the sacrifice of children on the altar of institutional reputation, are in clear violation of everything the Gospel stands for. There can be no place in positions of authority and influence for those who exploit the young.

Contours of a Crisis

Because the scandal has come in waves, it is worth briefly recapping the main stages of a developing crisis and the Church's response. The crisis itself has had three dimensions:

1. *The scandal of clerical sex abuse.* Revelations that a large number of priests had abused their status to manipulate and coerce young people into illegal and immoral sexual relations began to be made in the 1980s, although the Church did not develop a systematic response until after 2000. The statistical evidence is clear that clerical sexual abuse of minors increased from the mid-1960s through to the late 1970s; it then declined in the 1980s and to this day remains very low. Ironically, it was not long after this sharp drop in abuse allegations against priests, in the late 1980s, that victims started to step forward. They were generally in their thirties and forties, or older — a silent generation finding its voice in lawsuits and news reports. But the abuse itself had happened much earlier.

2. *A failure of local Church leadership.* What lay behind the firestorm of media outrage following the publication of the 2009 Murphy Report into abuse mishandling in the Dublin Archdiocese was the revelation that victims seeking redress from the Church in the late 1980s and 1990s had been rebuffed, paid off and silenced, while perpetrators went unpunished either by Church or civil law. There were many reasons for the bad decisions: a desire to preserve the Church's good name, a failure to understand the deceitfulness of sex abusers, belief in the power of therapy, as well as the difficulty many victims had in talking clearly and directly about their experiences. Although there is little evidence of deliberate concealment of evil, and plenty of evidence of ignorance, these failures are usually summed up in the word 'cover-up'.

3. *A failure of universal Church leadership.* In 1996 when the Irish bishops' conference adopted the first comprehensive Church framework for responding to abuse allegation, Rome was slow to act. The

Vatican refused to give the document official recognition and told the bishops that it was "not an official document of the Episcopal Conference but a study document"; and warned that it could be in breach of canon law. It also said the document's advice on mandatory reporting gave rise to "serious reservations of both a moral and a canonical nature". Judge Yvonne Murphy described the Vatican response as "entirely unhelpful". The Vatican showed itself initially tone-deaf and defensive following revelations of failures to force local bishops to take action against abusive priests, and even obstructional in the case of two particularly notorious cases of very senior abusers: the former archbishop of Vienna, Hans Herman Gröer, forced to resign in 1995, and Fr Marcial Maciel, founder of a global order of priests known as the Legionaries of Christ, who had no action taken against him in the late 1990s, despite formal charges being laid against him in the Vatican. From 2001, however, the Vatican began to deal comprehensively with the issue, after Cardinal Joseph Ratzinger, later Benedict XVI, took a lead role. Under the pontificates of Benedict XVI (2005–2013) and now Francis, Rome has taken the lead in ensuring that the Church worldwide becomes a leader in safeguarding, learning from the experience of the bishops in countries like Ireland.

The timeline is important. This is a crisis about the Church's response to abuse that took place — for reasons we will discuss — above all in the 1960s–70s. At the time, the abuse was almost never reported, either in the Church or in society in general. (It is the least reported crime on the planet, and to this day less than 1% of sex abuse of children leads to a conviction.) To describe this as a cover-up is extremely misleading, for it implies a deliberate intention to conceal information from those who have a right to know about it. It is also to read the past through the lens of the present. In an environment where there was barely the language to articulate it, the victims — usually silenced by their own emotions, the same that gag the adult victims of rape, but which are magnified in a child's mind — stayed quiet. When they tried to talk about it, they were not believed or were dismissed; this was behaviour typical of society as a whole at the time, especially of institutions such as schools or orphanages. Neither police nor the media saw it as an issue worth investigating. The Church's failure to hear the voice of the victims was neither unique nor exceptional — although it is reasonable to ask why the Church did not set an example on this issue at the time.

The reason is ignorance. The Church's failures mostly relate to the 1980s–90s, when victims did begin to step forward. But even then, bishops took a long time to come to terms with the scale and seriousness of the issue. In many cases, there is evidence that bishops didn't even speak to one another about the issue.

The most detailed report into the abuse in Catholic institutions was commissioned in 2002 by the US Catholic bishops from independent researchers, at a cost of US $1.8 million (€1.47 million). The highly regarded John Jay College of Criminal Justice in New York published the first part of its report, *The Nature and Scope of the Problem of Sexual Abuse of Minors by Catholic Priests and Deacons in the United States*, in 2004; the second part, *The Causes and Context of Sexual Abuse of Minors by Catholic Priests in the United States, 1950–2010* came out in May 2011.

The report examined all plausible allegations of abuse of young people by clergy in the period between 1950 and 2002. The researchers used a very low standard of proof for the charges — not withdrawn or known to be false — rather than proof of guilt. Over that fifty-year period, the study found that 4,392 out of about 100,000 clergy were accused — just over 4% of all priests. (A more accurate estimate of numbers of priest abusers, one cited by Pope Francis, is closer to 2%). About 80% of the accusations were of abuse alleged to have occurred between the 1960s and the 1980s; more than half of those accused were accused of a single incident; and almost all the allegations concerned post-pubescent males — in other words, they were not allegations of paedophilia *per se* (although no less criminal and sinful). Just 149 individuals were responsible for a quarter of all abuse allegations. And 40% of the allegations date from a six-year period in late 1970s.

The second part of the report revealed that by the mid-1980s, bishops knew that abuse had occurred, but they had no idea of its extent. "Though more than 80% of cases now known had already occurred by 1985, only 6% of those cases had been reported to the dioceses by that time," the report notes. The bishops simply did not know of the scale of the problem until much later — in fact, not until the 1990s. At this point they began to take action: in most countries, guidelines were drawn up by bishops' conferences. John Jay shows that while abuse increased in the Church at the same time as it increased in wider society, it decreased in the Church from the 1980s because of the actions taken by the Church at the time.

In the inadequate actions that it did take in the 1990s, the Church was in fact ahead of the curve. Society was only beginning to wake up to the reality of abuse. Amazingly, the 1995 UN Committee report on the Holy See's implementation of the Convention of the Rights of the Child makes no mention of the issue of sex abuse, instead rapping the Holy See's knuckles over issues that now seem risibly minor.

But while it notes that ignorance, rather than conspiracy, lies behind the inadequacy of the Church's responses, John Jay blames the bishops for being "typically focused on the priest-abusers rather than on the victims". They remained ignorant of the effect of sexual abuse because they did not often meet with victims before 2002; as knowledge of victim harm increased in society generally in the 1990s, so did the understanding by Church leaders.

"I think the bigger fault was that nobody would talk about it, nobody would mention it — I was certainly unaware of it," Cardinal George Pell, then Archbishop of Sydney, told an Australian inquiry in 2013. "I don't think many, if any, persons in the leadership of the Catholic Church knew what a horrendous widespread mess we were sitting on."

The real transformation in the Church only began when its bishops began meeting with survivors of abuse. Hearing their stories has been the main catalyst of conversion, turning bishops into passionate advocates of reform.

Cardinal Ratzinger, then head of the Vatican's doctrinal watchdog, the Congregation for the Doctrine of the Faith (CDF), underwent such a conversion in 2003. As a result of changes introduced by Pope St John Paul II two years earlier following complaints that bishops were stonewalling victims, the CDF became responsible for dealing with abuse crimes in canon law. The new legislation compelled diocesan bishops all over the world to forward their case files to Rome, to ensure that action was taken. More than 3,000 files landed in the CDF in 2003 and 2004. Msgr Charles Scicluna, a Maltese priest who served as the Promoter of Justice in the

Congregation for the Doctrine of the Faith — in effect, its lead prosecutor — has described how sitting down each Friday to read through victim testimonies left Cardinal Ratzinger devastated. Having sifted through the files, Ratzinger and Scicluna concluded that in most cases the evidence was so overwhelming that immediate action was required. Of the 500-plus cases that the Congregation for the Doctrine of the Faith dealt with prior to 2005, the substantial majority were returned to the local bishop authorising immediate removal from ministry and often expulsion from the priesthood.

After Cardinal Ratzinger became Pope Benedict XVI in 2005, the pace of reform increased: Maciel was sentenced to a life of prayer and penance from 2006 (he died two years later). Of the 3,400 cases reported by local dioceses to the Vatican between 2004 and 2011, 848 priests were laicised, while 2,572 received similar penalties to Maciel — usually old or infirm men who had served time in prison and had long been removed from active ministry. Visiting the US and Australia in 2008, Benedict XVI became the first Pope to meet with victims, scheduling such meetings into all his foreign visits thereafter; he also made public apologies to them on behalf of the Church. In 2018, it was revealed that Pope Francis sets aside Friday mornings in his private rooms at the Vatican for meetings with people who have experienced abuse at the hands of priests or religious. In 2011, Church law dealing with abuse was tightened still further, and bishops' conferences across the world were told to draw up guidelines for handling abuse allegations in the way that the Church in most Western countries, above all the English-speaking ones, already had. The Vatican directed them to ensure that victims were always treated with respect and listened to, that there would be no place in the priesthood for those who harm the young, and that all allegations were referred to the CDF and to the civil authorities. The following year a major Vatican summit sought to help bring every diocese in the world up to the level of those countries that had led the way on the issue.

What we see, therefore, is a *before* and *after* within the Church, at both the local and universal level. Before describing the path of reform since then, we need to understand better where the failures prior to that time lie — and to counter some myths.

Accounting for Abuse and Inaction

While it had been brewing for some time, in 2002 the crisis exploded in Ireland when RTÉ aired the Prime Time special *Cardinal Secrets* produced by Mary Raftery. The programme alleged that Cardinal Desmond Connell had concealed the fact that two priests had been dismissed from the clerical state due to allegations of abuse. It further claimed that the archdiocese had failed to given information about these former priests to the civil authorities and that the cardinal had written a reference for a priest alleged to have sexually abused a child. An earlier programme, *Dear Daughter,* in 1996 had also aired serious allegations of abuse and neglect in industrial schools and other state-funded institutions managed by religious orders.

The 2002 programme led to the setting up of a Commission of Inquiry and claims of the mishandling of abuse allegations began to emerge about other dioceses. What emerged was a sorry picture from the previous decades of inaction, denial, shuffling abuser priests between parishes, and the stonewalling of victims. The revelations meant that the story was rarely off the front pages.

In 2009, the Commission of Inquiry report (the Murphy Report) was published and concluded that Church authorities in Dublin had placed the reputation of the Church and the avoidance of scandal ahead of the needs of victims and their right to justice. In response, the Irish bishops' conference issued a statement in which they said, amongst other things:

> "We are deeply shocked by the scale and depravity of abuse as described in the report. We are shamed by the extent to which child sexual abuse was covered up in the Archdiocese of Dublin and recognise that this indicates a culture that was widespread in the Church. The avoidance of scandal, the preservation of the reputations of individuals and of the Church, took precedence over the safety and welfare of children. This should never have happened and must never be allowed to happen again. We humbly ask for forgiveness."

The bishops' public acknowledgement of past failings following the publication of the report was hailed by some as a new recognition of the problem. The truth is, however, the Church had been on a painful journey. In 2006, the hierarchy along with the Conference of Religious in Ireland (CORI) and the Irish Missionary Union (IMU) had already responded to public mistrust of the Church's handling of the issue. While initially, the bishops had sought to reassure Catholics that this issue was now being dealt with comprehensively, they now recognised that an independent body would be necessary. The National Board for Safeguarding Children in the Catholic Church in Ireland (NBSCCCI) came into existence as an independent watchdog. No longer would the Church be responsible for ensuring that it was following the highest possible standards, it would be assessed from outside. Under the initial stewardship of Ian Elliott – a northern Protestant – the NBSCCCI was and remains responsible for auditing how dioceses, religious orders and other Church institutions handle abuse allegations. The board is also responsible for ensuring that the highest standards are always adhered to in terms of the safeguarding of children and vulnerable adults.

The rate of abuse by clergy was less than that of comparable institutions and professions — similar to rates of abuse by male clergy of other denominations, considerably less than the male adult population in general, and much less than professional groups such as teachers. But the Church is unique in being a single institution as well as being a decentralised entity running a vast network of parishes, schools and agencies. Even though dioceses had very different records on their handling of the issue, it was easy for critics to paint a picture of an organised cover-up. To date, the Church has spent tens of millions of euro settling legal actions on behalf of victims and a similar amount in providing counselling and support to people abused by priests and religious – it is an ongoing work. As Archbishop Eamon Martin of Armagh has pointed out, the Church continues to journey with survivors and the issue can never be consigned to the past.

The John Jay report reveals that in the period of the 1960s–70s, between 1,000 and 3,000 priests in the United States sexually engaged with children, leaving as many as 100,000 total victims of clerical sexual abuse. In January 2014, Pope Francis spoke of "corrupt priests" who "instead of giving the Bread of Life, give a poisoned meal to God's holy people". He said those responsible "had a position in the Church, a position of power, even of comfort. But the Word of God, no!"

There have been many explanations. Some have blamed clerical celibacy, others the poor screening and formation of candidates for the priesthood back in the 1960s. Others, pointing to the fact that most (80%) of the victims were teenage boys, blame 'gay priests'. Others have pointed to the climate that permitted the deception and cover-up of abuse, attributing it to clericalism — priests having unquestioned authority — and the fear of scandal. Still others have advanced the 'Woodstock; hypothesis — the 1960s 'anything goes' atmosphere of sexual permissiveness that exploded taboos.

John Jay dismisses both the celibacy and homosexuality hypotheses. Most abuse is carried out by married men; if Catholic clergy are no more likely to be sex offenders than other clergy or men in general, then celibacy can't be a cause. And if there remain many gay priests (between 25 and 35%, according to studies), why is the abuse confined to the 1960s–70s? In any case, "same-sex sexual behaviour prior to ordination did not significantly predict the sexual abuse of minors," noted John Jay.

The study identified two types of offender: the genuine paedophiles who made up just 5% of offenders but who had a large number of (pre-pubescent) victims over a long period; and the opportunistic offender, who made up the overwhelming majority of abusers. In these cases, the victims were post-pubescent males, and fewer in number; in half of the cases, there was only one victim. The group that the study found was most likely to offend were those who could best be described as sexually confused, with psychological problems, who had often themselves experienced abuse, and who, under stress, replicated what had happened to them.

This was especially true of the offenders who had entered the priesthood prior to the 1970s, when screening of candidates was first introduced. Thomas Plante, professor of psychology at Santa Clara University, writes in his 2010 study, *A Perspective on Clergy Sexual Abuse*, that thirty years ago most priests entered seminary during high school, did not participate in a comprehensive psychological evaluation prior to admission, and had no training in sexuality, maintaining professional boundaries, or impulse control. "It is not surprising that the majority of the sex-offending priests that we hear about in the press are older. In fact, our research indicates that the average age of these men is 53."

The John Jay report blames the combination of the sexual revolution outside the Church and the widespread questioning of authority and discipline in the Church of the 1970s. The report argues that the decisive factor was the combination of inadequate seminary formation and sexual laxity in wider society, exacerbated by clericalism. This last factor was behind the poor handling by bishops, who did not act to stamp it out, partly out of fear for the damage it would cause the Church and partly out of ignorance: the prevailing psychiatric wisdom of the time was that abuse of children was an illness that could be managed or controlled with medication and therapy.

A common myth is that bishops resorted to canon rather than civil law in dealing with abusive priests and that canon law did not treat the abuse as a crime. In fact, it is a crime in both systems of law, and the record shows that bishops resorted to neither. According to the 2009 Murphy Report:

> "There is a 2,000-year history of biblical, papal, and Holy See statements showing awareness of clerical child sexual abuse.... Over the centuries, strong denunciation of clerical child sexual abuse came from popes, Church councils, and other Church sources. These denunciations are particularly strong on 'offences against nature' and 'offences committed with or against juveniles'."

The 1917 *Code of Canon Law*, for example, decreed "deprivation of office and/or benefice, or expulsion from the clerical state for such offences", the report notes. The commission goes on to report that "in the 20th century, two separate documents on dealing with child sexual abuse were promulgated by Vatican authorities". The documents, says the commission, were "little observed in Dublin". The report also notes that in Dublin "the Church authorities failed to implement most of their own canon law rules on dealing with clerical child sexual abuse". In a vindication of the law of the universal Church, the report notes: "The commission is satisfied that Church law demanded serious penalties for clerics who abused children. In Dublin, from the 1970s onwards, this was ignored." The report goes on: "canon law provides the Church authorities with a means not only of dealing with offending clergy, but also with a means of doing justice to victims, including paying compensation to them."

Canon law demands that a bishop investigate an allegation of sexual abuse and, if well founded, ask Rome to impose sanctions, including removing the abuser from the priesthood. Canon law also demands that the bishop refer the matter to local civil authorities. Yet neither happened in those cases where the bishop became aware of the allegations. In not having recourse to the law, the bishops were, again, acting typically for the time; it was virtually unheard of in the 1960s–70s for a school or other institution to call in the police to investigate sexual abuse of children.

Meanwhile, the use of the penalties in the Church's own law had fallen into disuse. After the mid-1960s in Ireland, notes Pope Benedict in *Light of the World*, ecclesiastical penal law "was simply not applied anymore. The prevailing mentality was that the Church must not be a Church of laws, but rather, a Church of love; she must not punish. Thus, the awareness that punishment can be an act of love ceased to exist. This led to an odd darkening of the mind, even in very good people." On this point, the Pontiff was quoting from information given to him by Archbishop of Dublin Diarumid Martin.

The Murphy Commission found that none of its four archbishops ever reported the abuse that was brought to their attention and that no canonical trials ever took place. The report documents a "collapse of respect for canon law...Offenders were neither prosecuted nor made accountable within the Church". This was not a specifically Irish phenomenon. Msgr Charles Scicluna, who was the Vatican's chief prosecutor for many years, has revealed that between 1975 and 1985 the Congregation for the Doctrine of Faith received no reports of abuse allegations against any Catholic priests.

The normal response was for a bishop to send an abusive priest to therapy, in line with the thinking of the time that paedophilia was a kind of psychological illness that could be cured. Later, it would be seen as a 'fixation' or 'orientation' that resisted therapy. The problem was not with the use of therapy *per se*, but the way it was used as an alternative to punishing acts criminal in both civil and canon law.

In his *Pastoral Letter to the Catholics of Ireland* on March 19, 2010, Pope Benedict XVI noted the specific failure of bishops "to apply the long-established norms of canon law to the crime of child abuse...Grave errors of judgment were made and failures of leadership occurred".

One of the reasons that bishops around the world typically did not apply to dismiss abusive priests from the clerical state during the 1980s and 1990s was that procedures were lengthy, cumbersome, and uncertain. Only after Cardinal Ratzinger's 2001 reforms was the procedure made automatic in cases where the evidence was overwhelming. The reforms were further tightened in 2010 — to the point where now a priest who commits abuse faces almost automatic laicisation.

These processes occur alongside — in fact, almost always after — the investigation, trial, and conviction of the abusive priest by the police of that country. Civil and canon penalties are not alternatives. They exist in two parallel spheres: each has jurisdiction the other lacks; each has its own judges and sanctions. Church law can dismiss a priest from the clerical state, which is not something civil law can do. A possible analogy — one easily understood in the professional world — is that of associations or clubs with their own internal regulations. A solicitor who commits fraud will be investigated by police and, if guilty, sentenced to a term in prison. But he will also be subject to punishment by the Law Society, which will withdraw his membership. Action or inaction in one jurisdiction does not prevent action or inaction in the other. The Church will often choose to pursue an allegation when the civil authorities have not. And even when the police have dropped charges against a priest, the accused priest must still go through a rigorous process of 'risk assessment' by Church-appointed experts before he is allowed back into his parish.

Why does the Vatican not mandate bishops across the world to report any allegation they receive to the civil authorities? The assumption of canon law is always that local civil law always be obeyed. As the Vatican's 2011 guidelines point out, "civil law concerning reporting of crimes to the appropriate authorities should always be followed." Rome urges the reporting of every accusation to civil authorities, but *mandating* such reporting would be impossible, because the Church operates in states where, for example, abuse of children is not a crime.

Ignorance of canon law, or the misreading of it to try to claim that the Church had a systematic policy of obstructing civil law, is at the origin of many of the false accusations against the Church in general. This includes a deeply flawed United Nations report in February 2014 that claimed child sex abuse in the Catholic Church had been dealt with in "confidential proceedings providing for disciplinary measures which have allowed the vast majority of abusers...to escape judicial proceedings in states where abuses were committed". The Holy See's procedures — bound by confidentiality to enable victims to give evidence — refer to canonical processes such as dismissal from the clerical state; they do not contradict, interfere with, or prevent in any way action under the civil law of states, and in general they demand that the civil law process of states be completed before canonical processes begin. If canon law allowed priests to escape civil judicial proceedings, how do we explain the clergy who have been imprisoned, or the tens of millions of victims paid out in compensation?

Reforms under Pope Francis

At the urging of Cardinal Seán O'Malley of Boston, in December 2013 Pope Francis created a new Pontifical Commission for the Protection of Minors to promote reform across the Church. It initially included the outspoken Irish survivor of clerical sex abuse, Marie Collins, as well as key experts and lay people, most of them women (although, Collins resigned in 2017 citing a lack of cooperation from some Vatican officials, underlining the need for constant vigilance on the issue). On their recommendation, in July 2014 Pope Francis invited six victims — two each from Ireland, Great Britain, and Germany — to tell him whatever they wished, one by one, over three hours. That morning, he celebrated Mass with them, asking for "the grace for the Church to weep and make reparation for her sons and daughters who betrayed their mission, who abused innocent persons". He added: "Before God and his people I express my sorrow for the sins and grave crimes of clerical sexual abuse committed against you. And I humbly ask forgiveness."

The Commission, later expanded to seventeen members, including other abuse victims, psychologists and experts from across the world, was tasked with developing best practice in a large number of areas: pastoral care for survivors, formation to priesthood, norms governing allegations, as well as the accountability of people in positions of authority in the Church who fail in their administrative obligation to enforce zero tolerance. Francis took a step in that direction when he ordered an investigation into Bishop Robert Finn of Kansas City-St Joseph, Missouri, who was criminally convicted in 2012 for failing to alert police to charges against one of his priests. In June 2015, he created a Vatican tribunal to judge bishops who failed to apply the Church's guidelines. Three US bishops, including Finn, as well as a Mexican bishop, stepped down in the weeks that followed.

In February 2018, Pope Francis appointed a new expanded Commission to reflect the global nature of the Church. The new members hail from Ethiopia, India, Australia, Tonga, the Netherlands, Italy, the United Kingdom, the United States and Brazil. They join members from the Philippines, Colombia, Germany, Poland, Zambia and South Africa. According to Cardinal O'Malley, who heads the Commission, "the newly appointed members will add to the Commission's global perspective in the protection of minors and vulnerable adults. The Holy Father has ensured continuity in the work of our Commission, which is to assist local churches throughout the world in their efforts to safeguard all children, young people, and vulnerable adults from harm." Victims/survivors of clerical sexual abuse are included among the members. According to a Vatican communique on the announcement, "since the Commission's foundation, people who have suffered abuse and parents of victims/survivors have been members. As has always been the Commission's practice, the PCPM upholds the right of each person to disclose their experiences of abuse publicly or not to do so. The members appointed have chosen not to do so publicly, but solely within the Commission. The PCPM firmly believes that their privacy in this matter is to be respected."

In February 2015, Francis wrote to all the bishops of the world and heads of the religious orders calling on them to align themselves with the work of the Commission. Convinced that "everything possible must be done to rid the Church of the scourge of the sexual abuse of minors and to open pathways of reconciliation and healing for those who were abused", he called them to ensure "there is absolutely no place in ministry for those who abuse minors". He also asked them to meet with victims and their loved ones, describing the meetings as "valuable opportunities for listening to those who have greatly suffered and for asking their forgiveness".

Safeguarding in Ireland

1. The independent watchdog the National Board for Safeguarding Children in the Catholic Church in Ireland (NBSCCCI) under the leadership of Teresa Devlin continues to monitor the implementation of stringent policies and procedures to ensure that the Church is ahead of the curve on the issue of safeguarding. Each diocese and religious congregation is constantly measured against seven standards to ensure that past allegations of abuse have been handled properly, fresh complaints are responded to, information is shared with the relevant authorities and those who make allegations are supported.

2. Every parish and Church-run body in the country has a dedicated safeguarding person who is responsible for ensuring that the highest standards are maintained.

3. Every priest, religious and Church volunteer is subject to vetting by Gardaí and the Police Service of Northern Ireland (PSNI) in the relevant jurisdiction.

4. Regular formal and informal meetings take place between dioceses and the statutory authorities to ensure that information is shared.

5. All dioceses and religious congregations have adopted safeguarding policies that exceed statutory responsibility and are monitored for compliance by the NBSCCCI. These spell out what is acceptable and unacceptable behaviour and encourage the reporting of suspicious behaviour. All dioceses have people appointed to liaise with people making allegations of abuse, whether historic or current.

6. Assistance to survivors is prioritised in all dioceses and religious congregations. The 'Towards Healing' service – which has been funded by the Church to the tune of tens of millions of euro – provides a counselling helpline, one-to-one and face-to-face counselling, family counselling, couples counselling, parent coaching,

practical workshops, psycho-educational groups, facilitated listening and advocacy services.

7. 'Towards Peace' has been launched to provide a safe supportive space where people who have been affected by abuse in a Church context can be accompanied as they seek their own experience of spiritual peace, one step at a time. The group has helped many survivors rediscover their deep faith that was damaged as a result of abuse.

8. All dioceses have committees and persons responsible for ensuring ongoing compliance with policies. The names and contact information of the coordinators are listed on diocesan websites and parish noticeboards.

9. Each diocese also has a review board — to which all allegations of abuse are reported — made up of people drawn from relevant professions such as police, probation services, social services, health and law. Religious orders have similar structures.

10. There is a 'zero tolerance' policy on abusers. When even a single act of sexual abuse by a priest or deacon is admitted or is established, the offending priest or deacon is removed permanently from ecclesiastical ministry, and, if the case warrants, dismissed from the clerical state.

As Ian Elliott, former Chief Executive of the NBSCCCI put it: "throughout and across the Church there are an army of trained volunteers who give freely of their time to create and maintain safe environments for children within parishes up and down the country. These people are learning more each year and increasing their competence to protect children and ensure that best practice is followed whenever concerns arise." He added: "at every level of the Church, people who occupy roles that bring them into contact with children are more aware of the dangers and risks that can exist for them. As a consequence, they are more ready to intervene and protect a child if they see them as being at risk."

▪ EXISTING FRAME

The Catholic Church, both locally and in Rome, ignored and covered up the clerical sex abuse of children by priests for decades and continues to do so, placing the preservation of the reputation of the Church and the impunity of perpetrators above the interests of victims. The Church is a dangerous place for children, and it should consider revising its rules on priestly celibacy as well as its instinct for dealing with the issue behind closed doors through its own internal legal mechanisms.

↻ REFRAME

The appalling crime of clerical sex abuse of children is a profound betrayal of priests' calling, the Gospel, and the community of the Church, and it inflicts deep and long-lasting damage that blights people's lives. For many years, the Church, like other institutions, and in common with wider society, failed to grasp the extent of sexual abuse and its compulsive nature; it mishandled accusations and failed to punish the perpetrators. But since the early 2000s, it has gone further than any other institution in Western society in ensuring those mistakes can never be repeated. Those reforms have made the Church transparent, accountable and one of the safest places for young people. The Church now recognises a non-negotiable principle of paramount concern for the well-being of children, which demands that Church officials always cooperate fully with abuse investigations by civil law enforcement, ensuring that no other interest can obstruct the functioning of domestic law in the country where an act of abuse has occurred. The Vatican has played its part by introducing automatic suspension and usually laicisation of priest offenders and by demanding that the Church worldwide follow the lead of the bishops' conferences of the English-speaking world in implementing avant-garde child safety norms. In a number of countries, among them Ireland, the Church's safeguarding procedures are recommended by government as a model for other voluntary institutions to follow. The system of safeguarding supervised by the NBSCCCI is exceptional, and it has been recommended as a model for other institutions to follow. Increasingly, that can also be said of the Church in other countries too. The Church has undergone a huge conversion in this matter and wishes to be a leading change agent in society, where awareness of abuse has yet to be translated into policies and procedures in many institutions. The key for those institutions — as it has been for the Church — is to listen to the experiences of survivors.

★ KEY MESSAGES

▶ Moral awakening. Society and its institutions have woken up to the prevalence of sex abuse of minors. Like other institutions 30–40 years ago, Catholic schools and parishes did not act on allegations and the survivors were not heard. There has been a sea change in the Church's attitudes and policies.

▶ Media has helped the Church to change. The media's job is to probe and to hold organisations to account, and they have shone a light on some dark corners in the Church, which has spurred the Church to change its attitudes and procedures.

▶ Priesthood is not a haven for abusers. The Catholic priesthood is not, nor has ever been, exceptional in the number of abusers in its ranks. There is no causal link between priestly celibacy and clerical sex abuse. The Church is now much more careful about who it accepts to the priesthood.

▶ No conflict between canon and civil law. All Catholics must obey the law — that's what canon law itself calls for. Both civil law and canon law regard the sexual abuse of minors as an extremely serious crime. They are parallel, not alternative, systems of law. The big difference between now and 30 years ago is that the Church now acts on both laws — reporting allegations to police and to the Vatican.

▶ The Church is a safe environment for young people. The system of safeguarding is exceptional and has been recommended as a model for other institutions to follow. Independent oversight is built in at every stage, and all allegations, however old, are automatically referred to police and social services. The Church runs a vast army of specially trained volunteers to help enforce the culture change.

Chapter 8

Lights at the End of the Road: *Resisting Assisted Suicide*

Challenging Questions

- Why does the Church oppose allowing people to choose the time of their own death?
- If a person of sound mind who is terminally ill and in dreadful pain wishes to die, why should the law prevent them by prosecuting those who assist them?
- Doctors have always helped people on their way to death; how is legal assisted suicide any different?
- What right does the Church have to tell people of no faith how they should end their lives?
- Opinion polls show that society is changing its mind about assisted dying. Isn't this another case of the Church trying to legislate its morality?

The drive to make it legal to help someone take his or her own life is one of the main ethical debates of our time, comparable, in its way, to the debate over legalising abortion in the 1960s. The US Supreme Court ruled in 1997 that states could prohibit physician-assisted suicide (PAS); there is no constitutional right, therefore, to ask a doctor to administer drugs that cause death. But PAS is legal in Oregon, Washington, Vermont and Montana, and many other US states are considering it. At either end of a decade, the emotional pull of stories of Terri Schiavo, a woman whose own family was split over her wish to die and was finally left to starve to death in 2005 after failed government attempts to intervene, and Brittany Maynard, who moved to Oregon to kill herself before her brain cancer did, became cultural icons of how not to die and how to choose to die, respectively. In 2014, *People* magazine profiled the last days of Maynard, a twenty-nine-year-old newlywed who legally took her lethal prescription a few weeks before Thanksgiving of that year.

Like abortion, the case in favour of assisted suicide is made by an appeal to a narrow ethic of autonomy: If a person is suffering unbearably, and wishes to end their life at a particular point, and in the manner of their choosing, who has any right to decide they can't? But the way the question is framed is deceptive. There is little, in practice, anyone can do to prevent someone determined to die by suicide. But the demand for assisted suicide is different: it is asking the law, and the medical profession, to recognise and enable that suicide. Not only does the decision involve others, notably doctors, it also requires changing the supposition of the law, which is the defence of life.

The call for assisted suicide reflects, of course, the rise of the ethics of autonomy to the exclusion of other ethical considerations. It is being driven by three main changes in society. The first comes from modern advances in medical technology, in which an ageing population means a greater prevalence of long-term, terminal conditions such as cancer, motor neuron disease, Parkinson's and Alzheimer's, which bring about great changes in a person and undoubted suffering. An ageing man or woman is now more likely to face years of incurable and long-lasting illness and suffering in a way that would have been unknown in previous eras.

The second factor is a decreasing familiarity with death and dying, which increasingly takes place in hospitals, which are poorly equipped to deal with it. With unfamiliarity comes fear.

The third factor is material prosperity, and with it a growing resistance to the idea of dependency and vulnerability, along with a desire for choice and control. It is not a coincidence that the legalisation of assisted suicide has occurred in wealthy countries. An individual's loss of capacities and abilities is especially traumatic in a high-achieving society in which people build their lives around usefulness, success and power. The question they, and society as a whole, face is whether such lives are less worth living once these vanish. Whatever an individual may (in passing, or permanently) conclude, what happens when our laws endorse that idea?

Until the 1960s, assisted suicide — or 'voluntary euthanasia' as it was then known — was one of the options advanced by the eugenics movement to help rid society of 'undesirables'. "The moment we face it frankly we are driven to the conclusion that the community has a right to put a price on the right to live in it," wrote the playwright and eugenicist George Bernard Shaw in 1934. "If people are fit to live, let them live under decent human conditions. If they are not fit to live, kill them in a decent human way."

Of course, advocates of legalising euthanasia reject the comparison with the eugenicists of the 1920s and 1930s who paved the way for the Nazi death camps; where eugenicists favoured compulsory sterilisation, abortion and euthanasia, the modern case for assisted dying rests, like that of abortion, on the 'right to choose'. Yet in both cases — the eugenicist call for euthanasia and the modern call for assisted suicide — a judgment is being made about the lack of worth of a human life. It may seem amazing now to recall that between 1915 and 1919 a Chicago surgeon, Harry Haiselden, publicly allowed six infants he diagnosed as hereditarily unfit to die by withholding treatment, and went on to make a movie, *Black Stork*, about a doctor who did the same (it was still being shown in American cinemas in the 1940s). In the case of an assisted suicide, a depressed or sick person is making the same decision about themselves. They have internalised the message that their life is not worth preserving. If the law condones that conclusion, what effect will that have on the way society views the elderly — or indeed the poor, the disabled or the unsuccessful?

In this context the Church once again represents a countercultural logic. In the world of antiquity, Christians cared for disabled children, rather than engaging in the practice of infanticide, and they stayed in areas afflicted by epidemics to care for the sick and dying, at risk to their own lives. The hope of the Christian message has always been that something of infinite goodness is possible even in the darkest of hours, even in the hour of death, and that in dying we learn the meaning of love and compassion. The hope of the Resurrection is the opposite of assisted suicide: it is not a longing to reverse or escape from physical death but to comfort and accompany the dying.

Such is the choice that assisted suicide poses to society.

✝ POSITIVE INTENTION

There are many positive values in the case for legalising assisted suicide, especially those that focus on compassion for those in pain and despair. It is compassionate to seek to help someone suffering serious pain, whether physical or emotional, to be free of it. Some people view their lives as so altered by suffering that what they endure obliterates everything else. Their suffering cries out to us. There is a positive intention, too, behind those who point to the many failings in the way the dying are treated in hospitals, sometimes with inadequate pain relief or being poorly cared for. The experience of seeing someone you love endure inadequate care can produce a fear of dying.

Why the Church Opposes Euthanasia

In common with a longstanding tradition of Western civilisation, the Church believes that dying naturally is a vital part of life's journey, in many ways the most meaningful part. Dying is a process of healing. Important things happen on that journey, and suffering and pain are often a part of it.

Dying is a highly meaningful gradual process of renunciation and surrender. Although some die swiftly and painlessly, it involves great suffering, because (and this is true of old age in general), it involves letting go of those things that in our lives we believe make us worthwhile and loveable: our looks, intelligence, abilities and capabilities. This is what the great Swiss psychiatrist Carl Jung called "necessary suffering", the suffering endured by the ego, which protests at having to change and surrender. The idea that this kind of suffering is a vital part of growth is not a uniquely 'religious' view, although Christianity — with the Cross and the Resurrection at its heart — has perhaps a richer theological understanding than most secular outlooks.

Yet while the Church sees a need to accept necessary suffering, it works to relieve and avoid what might be called 'unnecessary suffering'. The abandonment and renunciation of illness and dying require loving support and sophisticated palliative care. Excessive physical pain and the loneliness of abandonment can and should be avoided.

Church organisations, pioneered in Ireland, the United Kingdom and the United States in the 1950s by the hospice movement, founded by a Christian, Dame Cicely Saunders, have transformed the way society now cares for the dying. "Last days are not...lost days," Saunders declared. Rather than seeing themselves as burdensome and unwanted, people with terminal illnesses should be in circles of love and care where they will be valued and made comfortable. In Ireland, homes for the dying - what would become known as hospices – have existed for over 100 years. Founded by religious orders, they sought to ensure that poor people could die with dignity in a safe environment. Hospices meet the needs of the dying much better than hospitals, which are not geared to those who no longer need treatment (where hospitals 'cure,' hospices 'care'). In their 2002 document, *End of Life Care – Ethical and Pastoral Issues*, the Irish bishops note that "in caring for people who are dying, there are two extremes to be avoided: a. trying to keep people alive at all costs, even when it is clear that death is imminent and b. deciding to end the life of a person on the basis that his or her life is no longer worth living...Palliative care avoids both of these extremes in that it upholds absolute respect for human life, and acknowledges human mortality and the dominion we have over life. It is about maximising the quality of life remaining, while enabling patients to live until they die." Learning how to face this last stage of our earthly lives is one of the most important and meaningful things each of us will do, and caregivers who help people through this process are also doing enormously important work.

The Church's view is that hospices need to be extended and made more accessible, such that no one ever needs to die alone and in severe pain.

As the bishops' statement notes:

"Care of patients at the end of life is a continuum of palliative care and usually refers to the final hours or days. This focus on improving and maintaining the quality of a patient's life until the end is life affirming for the patient but also accepting of the inevitability, however unwelcome, of death. Palliative care embraces the principles of non- maleficence (not to harm deliberately) and beneficence (to do good), which are basic ethical principles in all health care practice. Hospice and specialist palliative care services aim to promote comprehensive care for those with advanced disease and a short life expectancy. While traditionally associated with death resulting from cancer, it is critically important that palliative care services are developed for the many who die from non-malignant disease, i.e., cardiovascular, neurological, and respiratory disease."

This is not, it should be clear, about extending a life unnecessarily. It is not right to zealously provide burdensome treatment to extend a life when it is disproportionate to the relief it brings. Pain management — a specialty of hospice care — may even, as an unwanted side effect, shorten a life. But if the intention is not to kill but to alleviate suffering, even when hastening death is foreseen, that is not euthanasia. The purpose of palliative care is to provide an environment of love and support for a person on his or her final journey.

But what of those who claim dying has no meaning beyond ending life, for whom the indignity associated with the process should at all costs be avoided, whether or not it involves intense suffering? Advocates of a change in the law see this as a classic case of religious people trying to impose their own norms on other people through the coercive power of the state. After all, they argue, an assisted dying law does not prevent anyone choosing, should they wish, to die a 'natural' death.

But the Church's opposition to assisted dying is not an attempt to persuade people of no faith to adopt a religious view of death. The Church's opposition relies on a view of the common good of society and how legalising assisted suicide would undermine that good. It argues that the effect of an assisted suicide law is directly to undermine the dignity of the dying. As the bishops put it:

"The argument that is used strongly to support assisted suicide is that life has value only so long as it has meaning for the person whose life it is and respect for 'self-determination' and 'personal autonomy' should entitle a competent person to decide for himself whether, when and how he/she chooses to end their life. The slogan 'right to die' has an appealing sound to it but few expressions are more poorly understood or are more misleading. The failure of such advocacy groups to realise that the greatest risks at the end of life are more likely to relate to inadequate services rather than over-intensive treatment yet again points to the need to ensure that education in ethics has a sound grounding in the evidence base of interventions and prejudice at the end of life."

In general when the expression 'right to die' is used people are usually seeking to establish a number of quite distinct claims, which are expressed in terms of the right:

⌘ to reject or to determine unwanted medical procedures including lifesaving treatment;

⌘ to commit suicide;

⌘ to obtain another's help in committing suicide, often subtitled a 'physician assisted suicide,' where doctors are the ones to administer the lethal dose or injection.

While the first of these four possibilities can certainly be regarded as a right, because there is a reasonable balance between the benefits and the risks involved, this cannot be said of the other three possibilities.

In 2011, the US bishops' conference published a reflection on the issue entitled *To Live Each Day With Dignity*. They point out that "the assisted suicide agenda promotes a narrow and distorted notion of freedom by creating an expectation that certain people, unlike others, will be served by being helped to choose death. Many people with illnesses and disabilities who struggle against great odds for their genuine rights — the right to adequate health care and housing, opportunities for work and mobility, and so on — are deservedly suspicious when the freedom society most eagerly offers them is the 'freedom' to take their lives."

They add: "Those who choose to live may...be seen as selfish or irrational, as a needless burden on others, and even be encouraged to view themselves that way."

Just as with abortion and capital punishment, the law cannot, in practice, be neutral: either the law regards death as a form of therapy, or it upholds the sacredness of all life. If participating in a suicide is legally and ethically acceptable, it can only be because there's a *right* to suicide;

and once the state declares such a right, the arguments for confining it to the dying will seem arbitrary at best, and choosing to allow God or nature to take its course would soon come to be regarded as optional, eccentric and even selfish.

These arguments about the effects of an assisted suicide law are not abstract, for there is now plenty of evidence in countries and states that have allowed it for those claims to be tested. What this evidence shows is that licensing assisted suicide in order to accommodate the wishes of a very small number of people is an illusion. In each case, the underlying dynamic of the law is changed — with lethal consequences. "We see evidence here not only of a practical slippery slope but a relentlessly logical slide," writes Dr Aaron Kheriaty in *First Things*, "from a cancer patient with six months to live to people who are merely unhappy, demoralised, dejected, depressed, or desperate. If assisted suicide is a good, why limit it to only a select few?"

In a backgrounder arguing *Always Care, Never Kill*, Ryan T. Anderson argues that assisted suicide does four unacceptable things:

1. It endangers the weak and the vulnerable. "People who deserve society's assistance are instead offered accelerated death."

2. It corrupts the practice of medicine and the doctor-patient relationship, by using the "tools of healing" as "techniques for killing".

3. It compromises the family and intergenerational commitments. Legal assisted suicide sends the message that those who are elderly or disabled are burdens. "Physician-assisted suicide undermines social solidarity and true compassion."

4. It betrays human dignity and equality before the law. "Classifying a subgroup of people as legally eligible to be killed violates our nation's commitment to equality before the law — showing profound disrespect for and callousness to those who will be judged to have lives no longer 'worth living,' not least the frail elderly, the demented, and the disabled." It makes arguing for a right to life incoherent as it becomes inconsistent.

Lethal Logic: A Warning from Belgium and Holland

These are not hypothetical fears. The dangers of the inevitable slide of this logic can be seen in the experience of physician-assisted suicide in Belgium and the Netherlands. After considering the evidence, Dr Paul McHugh, a professor of psychiatry at Johns Hopkins University School of Medicine, believes that "with physician-assisted suicide, many people — some not terminally ill, but instead demoralised, depressed and bewildered — die before their time".

In 2001, the Netherlands was the first country in the world to legalise euthanasia and, along with it, assisted suicide. Various 'safeguards' were put in place to show who should qualify, and doctors acting in accordance with these 'safeguards' would not be prosecuted. For five years after the law became effective, physician-induced deaths remained level — and even fell in some years. The experts reviewing the figures concluded in 2007 that there was no "slippery slope".

But it turned out that the stabilisation in the numbers was just a temporary pause. Beginning in 2008, the numbers of these deaths began to increase by fifteen percent annually, year after year. The annual report of the committees for 2012 recorded 4,188 cases (compared with 1,882 in 2002), and was expected to reach 6,000 in 2015. Euthanasia is on the way to become a 'default' mode of dying for cancer patients.

Professor Theo Boer, a Dutch ethicist who argued at the time in favour of a "good euthanasia law" that would keep numbers low, was one of those reviewing the figures who changed his mind. "Now, with twelve years of experience, I take a very different view," he says. He now believes that the very existence of a euthanasia law turns assisted suicide from a last resort into a normal procedure. After reviewing over 4,000 cases, he writes:

"Cases have been reported in which a large part of the suffering of those given euthanasia or assisted suicide consisted in being aged, lonely, or bereaved. Some of these patients could have lived for years or decades. Pressure on doctors to conform to patients' — or in some cases relatives' — wishes can be intense. Pressure from relatives, in combination with a patient's concern for their wellbeing, is in some cases an important factor behind a euthanasia request."

More than half the cases of physician-assisted suicide in the Netherlands are involuntary. Government surveys found that as many as 650 infants per year have been killed by doctors, including those deemed to be facing a life of severe suffering with no prospect of improvement. Few prosecutions have ever taken place, because the doctors have applied the logic of the law. If it's appropriate to kill someone with a terminal disease when they request it, is it so inappropriate to kill one who cannot express a view either way?

As Dr Ezekial Emanuel, a key adviser to the construction of the Obama administration's healthcare law, wrote in the *Atlantic Monthly*, "The Netherlands studies fail to demonstrate that permitting physician-assisted suicide and euthanasia will not lead to the non-voluntary euthanasia of children, the demented, the mentally ill, the old, and others. Indeed, the persistence of abuse and the violation of safeguards, despite publicity and condemnation, suggest that *the feared consequences of legalisation are exactly its inherent consequences*."

In Belgium, which legalised euthanasia in 2002, cases rose from 24 in 2002 to 1,432 in 2012. In 2011–2012, 75% of the cases were for cancer (including all malignancies), 7% were for progressive neuromuscular disorders (multiple sclerosis, amyotrophic lateral sclerosis, Parkinson's disease, etc.) and 18% were for 'other conditions'.

The trend is clear: euthanasia in Belgium and Holland has become part of normal medical care.

Doubling Down on Death in Oregon

In addition to eroding a general culture of life, euthanasia also corrodes due diligence in health care.

In the US state of Oregon, where assisted suicide has been legal since 1998, cases have gone from 16 in 1998 to 71 in 2011, to 133 in 2016, an increase of 831%. The reasons people take their lives under the state's *Death with Dignity Act* reflect existential issues around loss — of autonomy, of enjoyment of life's activities, of dignity — rather than pain, which doesn't make it into the top five reasons given. Fewer than six percent of the 752 reported cases of individuals who have died by assisted suicide under Oregon's law were referred for psychiatric evaluation prior to their death despite the fact that most suicides are associated with clinical depression or other treatable mental disorders.

Once suicide is seen as a good — and even celebrated (Brittany Maynard has been applauded for her "inspiring and courageous" example — one of CNN's 'Eleven Extraordinary People of 2014' — for choosing assisted suicide), it has copycat effects. At a time when suicide rates are the third leading cause of death for adolescents and young adults according to the Centres for Disease Control and Prevention, making suicide legal in any context threatens more than the sick and old: it threatens anyone feeling alone or like a burden. According to Oregon Public Health numbers, the state's suicide rates had declined in the 1990s, only to increase "significantly" between 2000 and 2010, "now 35% higher than the national average".

Prof. Des O'Neill, an expert in care for the elderly at Trinity College Dublin (TCD) and Tallaght Hospital who also heads the Centre for Ageing, Neuroscience and the Humanities, believes those arguing for assisted suicide are feeding prejudices against the old, disabled, ill and infirm that would not be tolerated against others. Questioning why assisted suicide seems to be societally placed on a higher ethical plane than other suicides, Prof. O'Neill notes that people are rightly horrified by how three times as many people die of suicide in Ireland as die in road traffic accidents, and yet there is a "determined failure not to link this with the tragedy of assisted suicide".

In a reflection he wrote six months before his death from cancer in November 2011, which was later published in the London-based daily *The Independent*, Christopher Jones offered his own experience to help British lawmakers decide whether to follow Oregon's example. He described the rollercoaster of emotions he felt following his diagnosis in 2009. After first being told he had colon cancer, he was then declared cancer-free, only to be diagnosed with cancer of liver just months later. Further operations revealed more tumours.

> "[A]t three periods — the diagnosis of secondary cancer, the traumatic experience of chemotherapy, and the prognosis of incurability — I was subject to extreme stress and a sense of hopelessness,

and I might have been open to the option of ending my life by legal means, had these existed. The legal prohibition of this course was immensely helpful in removing it as a live option, thus constraining me to respond to my situation more creatively and hopefully. In hindsight, I now know that had I taken this course, I would have been denied the unexpected and joyful experience of being 'recalled to life as I now am...'

"As well as prescribing sanctions when offenses are committed, law has directive and preventative effects. By setting boundaries, they help to maintain an environment of healthy ethics, good practice, and positive expectations. A nakedly individualist account of decisions about the ending of life neglects or underestimates this context. In the light of my experience, it is of prime importance that the law should signal the priority of the preservation of life — not at all costs but as the default option which requires adequate reasons to be overridden...

"A life-threatening or terminal illness is a process with many imponderable and unpredictable elements. There is great danger in attaching decisive significance to a person's judgment at a particular stage in the process that their life is no longer worth living and ought to be ended, as both the situation and their feelings about it may change drastically in a relatively short period of time...

"[M]y experience has reinforced my conviction that the law prohibiting assisted suicide is an essential bulwark against well-meaning but unwarranted judgments about the value of life and the desirability of ending it in order to minimise or eliminate suffering. In my view, suffering is inescapable in this situation, and ought not to be allowed to trump all other considerations, especially when palliative care is taken into account."

A Call for Better End-of-Life Care

The testimony of the widow of the late Democratic Senator Edward M. Kennedy was one reason why assisted suicide failed to become law in Massachusetts in 2012. In her op-ed, Victoria Reggie Kennedy painted a less rosy view of an assisted death than campaigners had suggested. "Most of us wish for a good and happy death, with as little pain as possible, surrounded by loved ones, perhaps with a doctor and/or clergyman at our bedside," she wrote. With assisted suicide, she wrote, "what you get instead is a prescription for up to 100 capsules, dispensed by a pharmacist, taken without medical supervision, followed by death, perhaps alone. That seems harsh and extreme to me."

Her husband was told he had only two or four months to live yet went on to live "fifteen months of cherished memories — memories of family dinners and songfests with our children and grandchildren; memories of laughter and, yes, tears; memories of life that neither I nor my husband would have traded for anything in the world."

It is axiomatic in the advocates' arguments that the individual must be the first and only judge of when the time is right for dying; and that those who feel they are a burden to others should be released from that feeling. This is consistently the major reason for seeking an assisted death. The Washington State Department of Health's annual report on its own *Death with Dignity Act* records that 61% of those who received lethal drugs in Washington in 2013 reported "feeling a burden on family, friends, and caregivers".

The question that needs to be answered, therefore, is this: Do we as a society wish to agree with those who consider themselves to be a burden, and kill them at their request?

Baroness Ilora Finlay, a British professor in palliative care and campaigner against assisted suicide, argues that people with such feelings are by definition vulnerable, and the vulnerable need defending. "In reality, the vast majority of people facing dying are ambivalent, oscillating between hopelessness and hope, worrying about being a financial or personal burden on those they love or that their own care costs will erode their descendants' inheritance. In a word, they are vulnerable, and it is a primary purpose of any law to protect the weak and vulnerable rather than to give rights to the strong and determined at their expense."

Keeping assisted suicide illegal is the best way of protecting the disabled, elderly, sick, depressed or other vulnerable people from ending their lives for fear of being a financial, emotional or care burden upon others.

But society must accept the implications of caring for the vulnerable. 'No' to assisted suicide is also a pledge to work for better care for the elderly and ill.

As Pope Francis told the Pontifical Academy for Life in 2015: "Abandonment is the most serious 'illness' of the elderly, and also the greatest injustice they can be subjected to."

Better care for the elderly means investing in hospice care, which since the 1970s has revolutionised the relief of extreme pain and raised standards for care of the elderly. The biggest threat to that improvement is assisted suicide.

In the Netherlands and Belgium, palliative-care provisions fall far below standards elsewhere. The architect of the 2001 Dutch euthanasia law, Els Borst, admitted in 2009 that the government of the time was wrong to have introduced euthanasia without improving palliative care. The Netherlands should be a warning to other countries. Persistent requests for euthanasia are very rare if people are properly cared for. But it's harder properly to care for people once euthanasia is allowed. Assisted suicide chills the environment for the dying, encouraging people to seek death as an alternative to the suffering they fear or the burden they are worried they will be on others.

Government programmes and private insurers may even limit support for care that could extend life, while emphasising the 'cost-effective' solution of a doctor-prescribed death. The reason for such trends is easy to understand. Why would medical professionals spend a lifetime developing the empathy and skills needed for the difficult but important task of providing optimum care once society has authorised a 'solution' for suffering patients that requires no skill at all? Once some people have become candidates for the inexpensive treatment of assisted suicide, public and private payers for health coverage also find it easy to direct life-affirming resources elsewhere.

Rather than defend the status quo, therefore, we need to be passionate reformers in the direction of improving the quality of the journey at the end of life.

Doctors and nurses who work in end-of-life care know that there are many myths about dying. One is that doctors 'speed up' the process by giving massive, fatal doses of morphine. In fact, morphine can extend life by controlling pain and breathlessness and making patients comfortable. Morphine does not kill. Just because there is the last dose of a drug does not mean that the drug causes death (you might as well blame the last cup of water). Equally, the removal of life support — apparatus to assist breathing or kidney or liver functions — does not cause death; when doctors decide to discontinue treatment it is to allow the process of dying to take place, because death cannot be prevented. An end-of-life decision is different from a life-ending decision.

Doctors are trained to understand and manage the all-important transition from, on the one hand, treating a patient — supporting a body's functions long enough to allow a person to recover — and, on the other, acknowledging that treatment is futile and no longer trying to block the natural process of dying. A doctor's role — supported by the Hippocratic oath — is to support life as long as life has a chance. There is no wonder the medical profession overwhelmingly opposes assisted suicide and euthanasia.

Perhaps the most potent myth — and one that drives the call for assisted suicide — is that deaths are painful and difficult, when most are not; or that deaths always require the prescription of opiate drugs, when they do not. In fact, most deaths are comfortable, if spiritually and emotionally demanding on everyone involved.

Sister Constance Veit of the Little Sisters of the Poor, who run homes throughout the world serving the elderly, says that the old person, writhing with pain, crying out for death is completely foreign to her three decades doing the work of caring for the sick and dying.

Yet deaths are not, on the other hand, 'dignified'. The advocates of assisted suicide appeal constantly to this idea of 'dignity in death' — as something rational and controlled, like a decision to jump into the sea before the boat hits the rocks. Dying involves renunciation, pain, and many indignities. We are not in control. And it calls forth compassion — 'suffering with' — in those who love and care for the person dying. Assisting a suicide is a corruption of compassion. A state that endorses it is creating an ominous new option that will rapidly undermine the sacred value of life itself. Rejecting it is the greatest act of compassion we can make for the elderly — while working for their real dignity.

■ EXISTING FRAME

A dignified death, free of pain, at a moment of our own choosing is now possible. Given that medicine now keeps us alive for years, why not use medicine to bring forward a painless death, ensuring that proper safeguards are in place? No one has the right to tell some-one suffering that they should prolong their lives, especially for peo-ple who have no religious view of death. In cases of terminal illness, when a person is depressed and feeling like a burden, why should they not be allowed to relieve themselves and others of the burden of staying alive, and opt for a dignified death? There should be a law to allow mentally competent, terminally ill people who see no point in suffering to choose the time and manner of their departure.

⟳ REFRAME

Assisted suicide is the wrong response to advances in medicine that prolong life. We need to spread palliative and hospice care that al-lows people to discover their true worth in spite of their illness and diminishment. Assisted suicide produces a logic of death that quickly corrodes society and the health-care profession. It makes the elderly and the disabled gravely vulnerable, while reinforcing messages that only the strong and successful lead lives worth living. Our response to those wanting to take their lives because they feel they are a bur-den should not be to confirm their suspicions, but to show them their true worth. That means working for truly dignified end-of-life care.

★ KEY MESSAGES

- ▶ Assisted suicide gives the green light to hopelessness and despair. It sanctions suicide as a response to hardship. The right to die becomes a duty to die.

- ▶ Assisted suicide leaves the vulnerable more vulnerable — espe-cially the disabled, whose lives may be judged less valuable in law. It destroys the trust between doctor and patient.

- ▶ Assisted suicide undermines palliative care.

- ▶ Suffering does not diminish a person's human value.

- ▶ Some suffering in life will be unavoidable; it is part of the process of dying. But we have the medical means to ensure people do not have to endure unbearable pain.

▶ The English-speaking world leads the globe in hospices and palliative care. We need more, not fewer, of these. People suffering/in pain should be offered real choice — the choice not to suffer unnecessarily, and to live their final journey as a time of spiritual healing.

▶ Rather than agreeing with those who believe they are a burden and killing them at their request, we should help people realise their worth and live lives of true dignity.

Chapter 9

Unfinished Business: *Women and the Church*

Challenging Questions

- Why does the Church think women aren't good enough to be priests?
- Why, when Jesus opened up new opportunities for women, has the Church sought to deny them a leadership role in the Vatican?
- Why is the Church such a patriarchal institution?

At the dawn of human history, male and female roles were rigorously divided. To men belonged responsibility, authority, and presence in the public sphere — law, politics, war and power — while women took charge of home, family and education. There were exceptional women who broke the mould, but the norm for most was pretty much fixed, especially in agricultural societies.

The division of roles had a philosophical underpinning: both the authors of the Book of Genesis and the Greek philosopher Aristotle believed that only the man provided fertile seed for generation; the woman was seen as the passive carrier. The contribution of ovulation by women took over 2,000 years to be discovered and verified by science. As the philosopher Sr Prudence Allen, RSM, observes:

> "In the history of philosophy, the lack of knowledge of a woman's equal contribution to generation with man led to a systematic, almost ideological, devaluation of woman's dignity for over two thousand years. The view of the male as naturally superior to the female permeated philosophical, scientific, and cultural attitudes. It harmed innocent women and girls in many hidden and other not-

so-hidden ways. Many of those who supported it were blinded to contrary evidence. Many men preferred to be thought of as naturally superior to women. In the last hundred years a reversal has begun to occur. Many women view themselves today as naturally superior to men. This has led them to adopt an almost ideological devaluation of man's dignity. But today the truth about women and men is well known. There is no excuse left to defend anything other than the equal dignity and significant difference of women and men."

At the same time, roles of gender and class were shaken up by eighteenth- and nineteenth-century industrialisation, mass migration, urbanisation, and social mobility. By the early twentieth century, women were demanding equality, including the right to vote and work, to be educated and access professions, to status and pay equal to men and to have a place in the public sphere as full citizens rather than as appendages.

Today many women seek to reconcile professional life with family commitments. But feminism, the movement for women's emancipation, is divided over deep-seated questions of identity and sexuality. Some believe that equality of dignity should not mean emulating men, but bringing about social changes that allow for women to preserve differences; equality, in this view, does not mean suppressing what makes women different from men. Others, influenced by new theories of gender, have sought to affirm that there is no difference between sexes: that gender is 'constructed,' and that fertility and childbearing constitute barriers to women's full integration.

Catholic women, with the support of the world's bishops at the Second Vatican Council, have been key advocates of the first kind of feminism, and usually in opposition to the second. They often find themselves caught between a feminist critique of the Church that is manifestly distorted, and a Church that still has a long way to go toward recognising the unique role of women in its structures.

The question of the Church and women is not just about the remarkable presence of the feminine in prayer and piety and the tradition of Christianity, but the place of women in the public life of the Church — and of Catholic women in wider society. That the Church has contributed, at times, to the marginalisation of women is not in doubt. Noting in his

1995 *Letter to Women* that "women's dignity has often been unacknowl-
edged and their prerogatives misrepresented; they have often been rel-
egated to the margins of society and even reduced to servitude", Pope St
John Paul II apologised for the times when "objective blame, especially in
particular historical contexts, has belonged to not just a few members of
the Church".

The Church is a particularly easy target for an anti-patriarchal critique because of the male priesthood and because key decision-making
roles are often reserved for the ordained. The charge against the Church
is not just that men are in charge, but that they are protecting their own
power interests. According to this view, the only way to overturn this 'patriarchy' is to begin admitting women to the priesthood.

Yet there are many prominent — successful by any standards — Catholic women who joyfully explain that there are sound theological reasons
for a male-only priesthood that are not about power and who question
the view of the human being implicit in egalitarian narratives. For them,
equality of dignity and status does not involve emulating traditionally
male roles, but allowing women's perspectives to be given equal expression in the Church. This was what Pope Francis himself called for in a
September 2013 interview when he said: "We need to broaden the spaces
of a more incisive female presence in the Church."

As a February 2015 gathering of women organised by the Vatican's
Council for Culture put it in its document *Women's Cultures: Equality
and Difference*:

> "[Women] often work, sometimes as top managers engaged as
> much as, if not more than, their male counterparts, and frequent-
> ly they also have to care for their families. They are women who,
> perhaps with great difficulty, have reached places of prestige with-
> in society and the workplace, but have no corresponding deci-
> sion-making role nor responsibility within ecclesial communities.
> There is no discussion here of women priests, which according to
> statistics is not something that women want. If, as Pope Francis
> says, women have a central role in Christianity, this role must find
> a counterpart also in the ordinary life of the Church."

✝ POSITIVE INTENTION

The feminist critique of society and the Christian tradition has its roots not only in the emancipatory ideas of the Enlightenment but also in the shift of consciousness that took place as result of the Incarnation. The divine equality of dignity of men and women — as well as their difference — is etched in the words of Genesis: "Male and female he made them." The search for genuine equality is the complementary expression of that divine revelation.

Women and the Church: A Brief History

The notion that a woman, like a child, is the property of a man was broadly shared in all ancient societies; this makes Christianity's challenge to that idea all the more remarkable. The Gospel opened new horizons for women. Luke's account of the Incarnation has women characters to mirror men's, while reversing their social roles: In Luke's narrative the men remain silent, are struck dumb, or ask to be dismissed in peace, while the women rejoice as God acts, speaking out and prophesying. The women of the Gospels, and above all Mary, recall many of the women hidden in the Old Testament who left their mark on history in spite of the best efforts of a male-dominated narrative. There is Miriam, who had equal status as a leader with Moses and Aaron in the exodus from Egypt, who sings the song of liberation (Exodus 15:21) later echoed by Mary; or Deborah, one of the divinely chosen leaders or Judges who led an army against Israel's enemy (Judges 4) — just as, later, St. Joan of Arc would lead troops into battle in fifteenth-century France.

Jesus was extraordinarily responsive to, respectful of, and indebted to women, and he counted them among his prominent disciples and dearest associates — Luke mentions Mary Magdalene, Joanna, Susanna, and "many others" (cf. Luke 8:2–3). Then there are various women with different roles of responsibility around Jesus, who — unlike the twelve apostles — did not abandon Jesus in the hour of his Passion. Among them, Mary Magdalene stands out in particular — the first witness and herald of the Resurrection.

It is a matter of record that Christianity was attractive to women and changed the way they were treated: the Christian sexual ethic, for example, differed from pagan standards in regarding a husband's unfaithfulness as no less serious a breach than that of a wife. And at a time when divorce was a male privilege — by the law of Moses, a woman could not divorce her husband — Jesus' insistence on marriage as a lifelong bond was a strongly pro-woman teaching. "Going beyond the social and religious barriers of the time, Jesus re-established woman in her full dignity as a human person before God and before men," Pope St John Paul II said in 1979. "Christ's way of acting, the Gospel of his words and deeds, is a consistent protest against whatever offends the dignity of women."

St Paul's doctrine that in Christ there is neither male nor female, free man nor slave (Galatians 3:28) did not question the social role of women any more than it actively sought to end slavery; but in elevating their status by insisting that they are created in God's image and redeemed in Christ and must therefore be treated with sovereign respect, he laid the foundation for their later emancipation. The modern movements for women's rights are the outworking of this principle.

In the early Church, women took on varied roles: teaching, preaching, prophesying, preparing for Baptism and hosting Church functions. The stories in the Acts of the Apostles of Lydia, the first baptised convert in Europe — and like Tabitha, a single woman — shows how in a short time the social roles had changed. Where the Gospel spread, women were among the first and foremost disciples, and they played crucial roles in developing the early Church. Across the first-century Mediterranean world, we find women being converted and serving the community in roles that would normally only have been available to them apart from the community. The historical evidence suggests, in fact, that Christianity spread firstly among women, slaves, and the foreign-born — precisely those excluded from public life — and through them to the upper classes.

This took place even as the priesthood developed as a male institution, based on Jesus' choice of men as apostles. The early Church regarded this as respecting Jesus' own mandate. Just as Jesus established the sacrament of Baptism with water, he established the sacrament of ordination using men. Restricting the priesthood to men is not to claim anything about male versus female abilities; it is obvious that women can exercise leadership and be good ministers — as Protestant churches show — but it does not follow that they can be Catholic priests. Given that Jesus and the early

Church opened spaces for women in spite of its patriarchal structure, and given that the 'priestess' was a feature of contemporary pagan religions, the choice is all the more remarkable and significant.

What is clear is that a male priesthood did not hold women back. This was most obvious in a new form of society that Christianity brought into being, monasticism, which challenged the existing forms of society in the ancient world in a host of ways. Monasteries involved physical separation from the ancient family and the city by an act of the individual will, a choice to live according to the universal principles of the Gospel. "In no sphere," observes Larry Siedentop in *Inventing the Individual*, "did this emerge more clearly than in the status and treatment of women." The creation of ascetic communities of women, which later became convents, he notes, "marked the emergence of women from the ancient family, from the permanent subordinations of the domestic sphere".

Women's roles became more prominent in the seventh, eighth and ninth centuries, when the expansion of the Church in Europe was led by the monasteries. More than thirty abbesses in just one country, Britain — among them St Hilda of Whitby and St Etheldreda of Ely — were acclaimed as saints by the early Church. They presided over often vast agricultural regions, established centres of learning, convened synods and led and guided huge communities of both men and women.

The point about these great women is not just that they were holy and inspiring, but that they were leaders in the modern sense of the word. Abbesses such as Hildegard of Bingen in Germany were consulted by bishops and popes, exercised very real authority, and had a huge influence, both through the offices they held and their gifts of teaching and preaching, over not just their own communities but the wider Church. If a male priesthood or the doctrines of Christianity led to the subordination and exclusion of women, it would have been impossible for this to happen. Yet great offices were held by women in the Church — just as they are today: the Focolare movement, established in northern Italy after the Second World War, and now numbering hundreds of thousands worldwide, has both men and women members, but by its own statutes must be led by a woman.

This is not to claim women in Church history have always been equal, or to deny that they have sometimes been excluded; but in spite of the obstacles of widespread patriarchy and misogyny in wider society, in the Church there could be prominent public women, and a male priesthood was not in itself an obstacle to them assuming such roles. In addition, the all-female religious communities of the Middle Ages offered opportunities for education and influence that were denied all but the most aristocratic women of the time.

Jesus' mother, Mary, the *Theotokos* ('God-bearer'), as well as the women disciples in the Gospel narratives, the virgin martyrs of the first centuries of Christianity, and the great women doctors of the Church (Catherine of Siena, Teresa of Ávila, Thérèse of Lisieux, and Hildegard of Bingen) all testify to the Church's deep respect for and appreciation of women. Catholicism has integrated the great gift of the feminine far better than other faiths or denominations. The great Swiss psychoanalyst Carl Jung praised the proclamation by Pope Pius XII of the Dogma of the Assumption in 1950 as the most important religious event in 400 years, re-establishing the feminine element in the human understanding of God's nature that had been rejected or downplayed in post-Reformation Christianity.

At the Second Vatican Council, the modern-day quest for expressions of women's equal dignity found expression in many documents. Noting how "women now engage in almost all spheres of activity", *Gaudium et Spes* said it was "incumbent upon all to acknowledge and favour the proper and necessary participation of women in cultural life". In *Pacem in Terris*, Pope St John XXIII too noted it was "obvious to everyone that women are now taking part in public life" and observed: "Since women are becoming more conscious of their human dignity, they will not tolerate being treated as mere material instruments, but demand rights befitting a human person both in domestic and in public life."

Blessed Pope Paul VI's documents contain some of the clearest unqualified statements about the rights of women to be found anywhere at the time, calling for the recognition of the civil rights of women as the full equals of men and for laws making it possible for women to fill the same professional, social, and political roles as men. That meant in the Church's structures, too, as Blessed Pope Paul made clear. "It is evident that women are meant to form part of the living and working structure of Christianity," he said in 1970, adding that "not all their potentialities have yet been made clear."

Women in the Church Today: An unfinished journey

Fifty years after the opening of the Second Vatican Council, Pope Benedict XVI reissued the closing messages issued by Blessed Pope Paul VI to people in various walks of life, including one to women, which ended with the plea:

> "Women, you who know how to make truth sweet, tender, and accessible, make it your task to bring the spirit of this council into institutions, schools, homes, and daily life. Women of the entire universe, whether Christian or nonbelieving, you to whom life is entrusted at this grave moment in history, it is for you to save the peace of the world."

By reissuing the message, Pope Benedict acknowledged that it hadn't been fully communicated and the world needed it as much, if not more, than it did at the close of the Council.

In recent years — since the Council and even much more recently — women have come to play a fuller role in the leadership of Church organisations. There were no women at all working in the Roman Curia before 1952, but by the end of Pope St John Paul II's pontificate in 2005, according to a Catholic News Service report women made up 21% of Vatican personnel. At a meeting with the clergy of Rome in 2006, Pope Benedict XVI said it was right "to ask whether in ministerial service...it might be possible to make more room, to give more offices of responsibility to women". By 2015, the number of women working in the Vatican City State had doubled (371 in 2014, up from 194 in 2004), although most of these are in service jobs, while in the Holy See in 2014 there were 391 women, up from 288 three years earlier, 40% of whom worked in professional positions. The proportion, in both cases, remained about the same (20%) as in 2005. There were only two women in decision-making roles, both serving as undersecretaries.

That is too few, although percentages of women at top levels in the business world are not very different. In February 2018, just 32 of the CEOs at Fortune 500 companies were women, a number that had barely increased since 2005. In 2018, nearly two thirds of Irish companies surveyed had fewer than 30% of board members who were women, and more than a quarter admitted that female boardroom representation was less than 10%.

The paucity of women in the Vatican reflects the relative scarcity of decision-making roles open to lay people due to the conflation of power of governance with ordination. In other words, what can look like male dominance is in reality clerical dominance. This is especially true in the Vatican, where positions of responsibility have been traditionally occupied by priests, even in roles for which sacramental power is not a prerequisite. The Vatican, in this sense, is very much a 'clerical club' — one of Pope Francis' great concerns — and its current structures reflect that, something that is set to change with the curial restructuring currently being designed by Francis' Council of Nine Cardinals, or C9. One of the principles of that reform is that only roles that specifically demand a priest should be filled by one, opening all others to lay people, including, of course, women. The C9's president, Cardinal Oscar Rodríguez de Maradiaga, notes: "The Spirit is pushing in this direction. More and more lay men and women are taking the joint responsibility of being leaders in the Church."

Down on the ground, in dioceses, where most Catholics live, there is plenty of evidence that the Church is ahead of the rest of society in women occupying leadership roles. In Ireland, women are the backbones of many parishes and diocesan administrations. At the Columba Centre – the headquarters of the Irish bishops' conference – the vast majority of employees are women. Women also occupy key administrative and teaching roles in parishes. In the Dublin Archdiocese – where the network of pastoral workers is the most extensive – well over half of these workers are women. Women are moving into ministerial roles within the Church "at rates which often surpass those of comparable institutions in the secular world", according to John Allen's 2009 book, *The Future Church*. Looking at current trends, he predicts: "In the trenches, the sociological reality is likely to be that the bulk of pastoral care offered by Catholic parishes, hospitals, schools, and other institutions will be delivered by women. Aside from the priesthood and the episcopacy, ministry in the Catholic Church will progressively become 'women's work'."

Vatican figures show that the total number of clergy and laity involved in the Church's apostolate went from 1.6 million in 1978 to 4.3 million in

2015, about 90% of whom were laypeople. This means that the number of laypeople occupying ministerial positions in the Catholic Church world-wide now exceeds the number of clergy by a larger and ever-increasing margin. The vast majority of these ministerial posts — teacher, catechist, pastoral worker — are occupied by women.

But most Catholic women do not work for the Church. Many are to be found at the highest levels of public life. Far from being inhibited by their faith from assuming those roles, many cite their faith as their motivation for engagement at home, in their parish community and in the broader world. Many more women give witness in other, more hidden ways. In *Breaking Through: Women Speak for Themselves*, Kim Daniels celebrates the life of a woman who had recently died in her parish, who had nine children and 23 grandchildren.

> "She did something else that was profoundly countercultural, and also particularly Catholic: She rooted her life in a particular place, and she stayed there. By committing to a parish, she and others like her helped build a robust community that people can count on. They can count on a thriving school to educate their kids; they can count on a place to serve others in their own neighbourhood; they can count on the possibility of true and long-lasting friend-ships in an increasingly transient and dislocated place. Because parishes by their nature root the sacred in the everyday — because the holy sacrifice of the Mass takes place right after the school bell rings, and right before the bazaar gets planned in the basement — holiness becomes a visible part of daily life."

The challenge is increasingly how to blend access to work (which many women cannot give up) with obligations to the family (which wom-en do not wish to give up and the family cannot afford for them to give up). As Pope Francis put it in January 2014: "How can one increase an effective presence in so many areas of the public sphere, in the world of work and in the places where the most important decisions are taken, and at the same time maintain a presence and preferential and wholly special attention to the family?"

Why Catholic Priests Are Men

Because a male priesthood is not a matter of discipline but a core doctrine of the Church, the question of admitting women to the Catholic priesthood is academic. Various popes have made clear that the choice of men as priests belongs to the deposit of faith, which it is the Church's mission to uphold. There is no power or mechanism by which it could admit women to the priesthood; the Church is 'powerless' to do so. Pope St John Paul II said in 1994 that "the Church has no authority whatsoever to confer priestly ordination on women" and noted that this was "to be definitively held by all the Church's faithful". Popes do not make such declarations unless they are sure they will not be contradicted in the future.

Because so many other Christian traditions — among them Lutherans, Episcopalians, Methodists, and Baptists — now have female clergy, the Catholic and Orthodox Churches look out of step. Consider each Church's view of the Eucharist and priesthood, however, and the divergence is not so surprising. The Catholic and Orthodox conception of the priesthood is very strongly Eucharistic and sacramental. Both Churches believe that an ontological shift takes place at the altar, and that a priest acts *in persona Christi*. The reference point, therefore, is Christ himself; and his maleness is not incidental.

The *Catechism* points out — with plentiful scriptural references — that "the Lord Jesus chose men (*viri*) to form the college of the twelve apostles, and the apostles did the same when they chose collaborators to succeed them in their ministry. The college of bishops, with whom the priests are united in the priesthood, makes the college of the twelve an ever-present and ever-active reality until Christ's return. The Church recognises herself to be bound by this choice made by the Lord himself. For this reason the ordination of women is not possible". (CCC 1577)

Reserving the priesthood to men is not a judgment on women's abilities or rights, any more than celibacy is a judgment on marriage, or marriage a judgment on single people. The teaching reflects the specific role of the priest in the Catholic understanding, which is to represent Jesus, to stand in his place.

As Pope St John Paul II wrote in his *Letter to Women*: "These role distinctions should not be viewed in accordance with the criteria of functionality typical in human societies. Rather they must be understood according to the particular criteria of the sacramental economy, i.e., the economy of 'signs' which God freely chooses in order to become present in the midst of humanity."

What 'sign' does a male priesthood give? The priesthood is not a career or a job, but a calling, a vocation, and a state of life. And while priests do exercise power — both the power to celebrate sacraments and the power of governance — they are called to do so in a way very different from a patriarchal model. It is possible to speculate, therefore, that one reason why Jesus called men to be priests is that he sought to create a model of male authority that involved service, self-emptying, vulnerability and openheartedness.

And in so doing, Jesus opened up another kind of power for women. A woman, as much as a man, and in ways that men cannot, can witness to the love of Christ and bring others to Him through her example and ministry. All Christians are part of the common priesthood. All are called to holiness. Being a priest or bishop does not make a person more holy. But the Church holds that only a man can represent Jesus in his humanity, a humanity that is not sexually neutral.

When Pope St John Paul II chose new patron saints for Europe — rulers, prophets and academics — half were women who had a profound impact on the era they lived in. St Bridget of Sweden was a formidable mystic and leader; St Catherine of Siena publicly admonished the Pope; St Edith Stein was a leading German philosopher of the early twentieth century. The Church is not afraid of the abilities of women; it was the Church that first set up schools in Europe to educate them. In the US, women (many of them religious sisters) built the backbone of America's schools and hospitals in the twentieth century. Looking at the Church across the globe, it is hard not to conclude that women drive the great Catholic enterprises that witness to Christ's love for humanity; and they do not need to be priests to do it.

A New Feminism

The Church has seen the women's liberation movement as positive in so far as it represents the coming-of-age of an essentially Christian impulse — the equal worth and dignity of women. While defending women's rights, however, Pope St John Paul II highlighted how women are different from men. Women and men have complementary natures, he taught, and their "diversity of roles" in the Church and in the family reflects that reality.

This idea of an 'integral complementarity' between the sexes is a basic tenet of the new feminism pioneered by Catholics responding to Pope St John Paul's call. "Discrimination is an evil," says Katrina Zeno in *Every Woman's Journey*, "but distinction is God's design." Men and women are different, and this difference affects the way they live their lives, what they care about and their strengths and weaknesses. But those differences should never be used to unilaterally discriminate except in cases where a task is subjectively contingent upon a person being of a certain sex (which for Catholic and Orthodox Christians includes the priesthood).

Equality for women must therefore include a respect for their difference. In his 1995 *Letter to Women*, for example, Pope St John Paul II called for changes to make women's equality a reality in the world: not just equal pay for equal work, but protections for working mothers; women who chose to have children, for example, should not be penalised in their careers for that choice. And he called for women who are "present and active in every area of life — social, economic, cultural, artistic, and political" — to help develop "a culture which unites reason and feeling" as well as "economic and political structures ever more worthy of humanity".

The new feminists oppose abortion and contraception not only because these are wrong (see Chapter 6), but because these so-called 'gains' for women in reality entrap them further within structures that compound their lack of freedom. New feminists believe that true solidarity with women requires that the underlying causes that make a child unwanted be challenged, not presumed.

This ambition, of working for a civilisation in which life is welcomed and protected, is the real route to women's freedom. For a woman to abort a child is to deny her own nature as a protector of growth and an enabler of life. There are many other acts of violence on women and their bodies: genital mutilation, crimes of honour, forced marriages, trafficking of women, sexual molestation, rape — which in some parts of the world are inflicted on a massive level and along ethnic lines — and are some of the deepest injuries inflicted daily. Domestic violence is the main cause of death in the world for women aged between 16 and 44. According to UN statistics, 70% of those who live in poverty worldwide are women. Catholic feminism pays particular attention to the disproportionate burden carried by women in war and conflict across the world.

Finally, the new feminism looks to the collaboration of the sexes and the ideas of complementarity and reciprocity. Where some twentieth-century feminism saw men and women as rivals, locked in a power struggle, new feminism regards the two genders as called to allow each other to become more fully who they are intended to be — as expressions of God's nature. The difference is that in this new feminism, the equality of women is not against men, but with them. What is now called for, in society and in the Church, is a better integration of the feminine.

▣ EXISTING FRAME

The gains for women in the twentieth century were achieved in spite of the legacy of Christianity, which has throughout its history oppressed women while lauding them as virgins and mothers. The Catholic Church continues that patriarchal legacy today by maintaining a gender ban on the priesthood, which sends a message of inferiority to Catholic women.

↻ REFRAME

The dynamic behind the emancipation of women comes from Christianity, as the history of the early Church shows. The Church has not been immune to patriarchy, but women have played and continue to play a vital role in the Church's leadership and ministries. The emancipation of women has been recognised and encouraged by the modern Church as well as in it: there are far more women in leadership roles in the Church than in comparative institutions. But equality must not be attained at the expense of what makes women different. The particular gifts and capacities of women are needed both in the Church and in society in order to humanise and transform society.

★ KEY MESSAGES

▶ Christianity laid the foundations for the modern emancipation of women by insisting on their equal worth and dignity. The early Church opened up new horizons for women, including social and public roles — although social pressures closed many down.

▶ Women have always played a vital, irreplaceable role in the life of the Church, and they continue to do so today.

▶ Although the Church, along with other institutions, has been too slow in overcoming barriers that exclude women, today it compares very favourably with secular society in the numbers of women in decision-making roles.

▶ The Church reserves priesthood to men because it has always seen Christ's choice as significant and binding, not because of any judgment on women. To see this as discrimination is failing to understand the true nature of what a priest is.

▶ Inspired by Pope St John Paul II's thinking, modern Catholic women have pioneered a 'new feminism' that seeks to emancipate women while safeguarding their distinct identity.

▶ The call now is for the Church to better integrate women by 'de-clericalising' its structures.